Everyone prays.
But no one finds it easy.
We all need a little help.

Pete Greig has been teaching on prayer – and leading a non-stop prayer movement – for more than twenty years. Now, for the first time, he puts his life's work into a response to the question everybody ultimately asks: how do I pray?

This down-to-earth introduction to life's greatest adventure will guide you deeper in your relationship with God, helping you to become more centred and still, clearer in discerning God's voice, more able to make sense of your disappointments and more expectant for miraculous breakthroughs too. It's full of honest, hard-won wisdom interspersed with real-life stories – some humorous, others moving – to equip and inspire your prayer life. Journeying through the Lord's Prayer, and accompanied by online videos from *The Prayer Course*, which has been used by more than a million people, it unpacks nine essential aspects of prayer: stillness, adoration, petition, intercession, perseverance, contemplation, listening, confession and spiritual warfare.

From one of today's most thoughtful and visionary communicators, for those who've been praying for years as well as those who want to pray but don't know where to begin, *How to Pray* is the simple, life-changing guide we've all been waiting for.

ALSO BY PETE GREIG

Dirty Glory

God on Mute

Red Moon Rising

HOW TO PRAY

A SIMPLE GUIDE
FOR NORMAL PEOPLE

Pete Greig

HODDER &
STOUGHTON

First published in Great Britain in 2019 by Hodder & Stoughton
An Hachette UK company

6

Copyright © Pete Greig, 2019
Foreword © Nicky Gumbel

Unless indicated otherwise, Scripture quotations are taken from
the *Holy Bible*, New International Version (Anglicised edition). Copyright
© 1979, 1984, 2011 by Biblica Inc.® Used by permission. All rights reserved.

Scripture quotations marked MSG are taken from *The Message*.
Copyright © 1993, 1994, 1995, 1996, 2000, 2001, 2002.
Used by permission of NavPress Publishing Group.

Scripture quotations marked NLT are taken from the *Holy Bible*,
New Living Translation, copyright © 1996, 2004, 2015 by Tyndale House
Foundation. Used by permission of Tyndale House Publishers, Inc.,
Carol Stream, Illinois 60188. All rights reserved.

Scripture quotations marked ESV are from the *Holy Bible*, English Standard
Version ©, copyright © 2001 by Crossway Bibles, a publishing ministry of Good
News Publishers. Used by permission. All rights reserved.

'Discipleship Today' from *The Signature Of Jesus* by Brennan Manning, copyright
© 1988, 1992, 1996 by Brennan Manning. Used by permission of WaterBrook
Multnomah, an imprint of Random House, a division of Penguin Random House
LLC. All rights reserved.

'Praying' from *Thirst* © 2006 by Mary Oliver

A CIP catalogue record for this title is available from the British Library

Trade Paperback ISBN 978 1 529 37492 6
eBook ISBN 978 1 529 37793 4

Typeset in Celeste and Gotham by
Palimpsest Book Production Ltd, Falkirk, Stirlingshire

Printed and bound in Great Britain by Clays Ltd, Elcograf S.p.A.

Hodder & Stoughton policy is to use papers that are natural, renewable
and recyclable products and made from wood grown in sustainable forests.
The logging and manufacturing processes are expected to conform
to the environmental regulations of the country of origin.

Hodder & Stoughton Ltd
Carmelite House
50 Victoria Embankment
London EC4Y 0DZ

www.hodderfaith.com

To Danny,
on his eighteenth birthday

'But you, man of God . . .
pursue righteousness, godliness, faith,
love, endurance and gentleness.
fight the good fight of the faith.'
(1 Tim. 6:11–12)

I will tell you as best I can how I approach prayer.
May our dear Lord grant to you,
and to everybody, to do it better than I.

(Martin Luther in a letter to his
barber Peter Beskendorf, Spring 1535)[1]

OUR FATHER IN HEAVEN,
HALLOWED BE YOUR NAME,
YOUR KINGDOM COME,
YOUR WILL BE DONE,
ON EARTH AS IN HEAVEN
GIVE US TODAY OUR DAILY BREAD.
FORGIVE US OUR SINS
AS WE FORGIVE THOSE WHO SIN AGAINST US.
LEAD US NOT INTO TEMPTATION
BUT DELIVER US FROM EVIL.
FOR THE KINGDOM, THE POWER,
AND THE GLORY ARE YOURS
NOW AND FOREVER.
AMEN.

THE ALTERNATIVE SERVICE BOOK
OF THE CHURCH OF ENGLAND

Contents

HEROES OF PRAYER

Foreword
Nicky Gumbel

I am so glad that Pete Greig has written this book. Prayer is the most important activity of our lives. It is the way in which we develop a relationship with our Father in heaven. Jesus prayed, and taught us to do the same. Prayer brings us peace, refreshes our soul, satisfies our spiritual hunger and assures us of our forgiveness. Prayer not only changes us, it also changes situations. God answers prayer. But *how* should we pray?

For many years, I have been hoping that someone would write a simple but comprehensive book on how to pray. The only ones I could find were written decades ago and had not stood the test of time.

There seemed to be a big gap in the market. On Alpha we have a talk around week five on why and how to pray. We like to recommend books, but have struggled to find one to recommend relating to this session about prayer. For the last few years I have recommended Pete's earlier book, *God On Mute*. But that is on a more specialised aspect of prayer – why some prayers do not appear to be answered. Nevertheless, I have recommended it because Pete is a legend in the world of prayer – having co-founded the 24–7 Prayer Movement – and he combines his passion for prayer with a remarkable gift of writing.

Imagine my joy, then, when Pete told me he was writing a book with the title *How to Pray*. I was deeply honoured when he then asked me if I would write the foreword for it.

Now, having read the manuscript, I find the book is everything I longed for and more. This is a writer who knows what he's talking about. He writes as he speaks – with great eloquence.

He is articulate but easily understood, immensely practical, illustrating his points beautifully with interesting anecdotes, stories and examples.

Pete used to lead the prayers at Holy Trinity Brompton so I have personally experienced the power of Pete's prayers – both for myself and for our church, the nation and the world. If, like me, you have tried leading corporate prayer, you will know how extraordinarily difficult it is to do it well. Pete always does it with consummate skill – with humour but never with intensity; with power and authority, but also with a lightness of touch.

This is indeed a book that does what it says – it explains *how* to pray. I, for one, have been greatly helped by it already, and I'm sure that everyone who reads it will be encouraged and helped to pray more like Jesus – and get to know God better.

Here at last is a simple guide to prayer for normal people – the book I have been waiting for.

Nicky Gumbel, HTB, London 2019

How to Read this Book in a Couple of Minutes

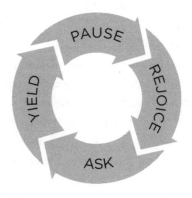

How to P.R.A.Y. (Chapters 1–2) – *'The disciples said: "Lord, teach us to pray!"'*

Every pilgrim gets a stone in their shoe eventually. You wake up one morning thinking, 'Is this really all there is to knowing the Creator of 100 billion galaxies?' You read the book of Acts and ask, 'Why isn't it like that any more?' Your world falls apart and you desperately need a miracle. You stare up at the stars and feel things bigger than religious language. You say to yourself, 'If this thing is *true* there's got to be more power, more mystery, more actual personal experience.' And so, finally, you turn to God, half wondering whether you're any more than half-serious and say, 'Lord, teach me to pray.' And he replies, 'I thought you'd never ask!'

PAUSE (Chapter 3) – *'Jesus said, 'When you pray . . .'*

To start we must stop. To move forward we must pause. This is the first step in a deeper prayer life: put down your wish-list and wait. Sit quietly. 'Be still and know that I am God' (Ps. 46:10). Become fully present in place and time so that your scattered senses can re-centre themselves on God's eternal presence. Stillness and silence prepares your mind and primes your heart to pray from a place of greater peace, faith and adoration. In fact, it is in itself an important form of prayer.

REJOICE (Chapter 4) – *'Say, "Our Father in heaven, hallowed be your name."'*

No one stares up at the Northern Lights thinking, 'Wow, I'm incredible!' We are hardwired to wonder and therefore to worship. The Lord's Prayer begins with an invitation to adoration: 'Our Father in heaven, hallowed be your name.' Having paused to be still at the start of a prayer time, the most natural and appropriate response to God's presence is reverence. Try not to skip this bit. Hallowing the Father's name is the most important and enjoyable dimension of prayer. Linger here, rejoicing in God's blessings before asking for any more. Like an eagle soaring, a horse galloping or a salmon leaping, worship is the thing God's designed you to do.

ASK (Chapters 5–7) – *'Your kingdom come, your will be done . . . and give us this day our daily bread.'*

Prayer means many things to many people, but at its simplest and most immediate it means asking God for help. It's a soldier begging for courage, a football fan at the final, a mother alone in a hospital chapel. The Lord's Prayer invites us to ask God for everything from 'daily bread' to the 'kingdom come', for ourselves ('petition') and for others ('intercession'). In this section, we explore the extraordinary, miracle-working power of prayer, but also the questions we face when our prayers go unanswered.

YIELD (Chapters 8–12) – *'Forgive us our sins as we forgive those who sin against us, and lead us not into temptation but deliver us from evil . . . Amen!'*

The final step in the dance of prayer is surrender. It's a clenched fist slowly opening; an athlete lowering himself into an ice-bath; a field of California poppies turning to the sun. We yield to God's presence 'on earth as it is in heaven' through *contemplative prayer* and by *listening* to his word, which is 'our daily bread'. We yield to God's holiness through *confession* and *reconciliation*, praying 'forgive us our sins as we forgive others'. And we yield to his power in *spiritual warfare*, asking our Father to 'deliver us from evil'. And so, in all these ways, it's by surrendering to God that we overcome, by emptying ourselves that we are filled, and by yielding our lives in prayer that our lives themselves can become a prayer – the Lord's Prayer – in the end.

Introduction

How to make the most of this book

With a God like this loving you,
you can pray very simply. Like this . . .
(Matthew 6:9, MSG)

When one of our sons heard that I was writing a book about how to pray, he said, 'Oh, but that's easy. You just say, "Dear God", chat to him for a bit, and then say Amen.'

In a way, he was right. Sometimes we make prayer way more complicated than it needs to be. *How to Pray* has been written as 'a simple guide for normal people'. It's an introduction to a vast subject aimed at new Christians and ordinary followers of Jesus who may not have studied theology and don't consider themselves ninja prayer warriors, but who would still quite like to grow and go a bit deeper in their relationship with God. It's going to be a wild and wonderful journey of discovery.

* * *

I am fortunate to live on the edge of open countryside where I often walk through the woodlands, around the golf course, or up to the top of the hill where you can see for thirty miles. There is a track I follow when I'm pushed for time, or if it's raining and I want to avoid the worst of the mud. But tangled around this main artery there are veins and capillaries – secret tracks and overgrown trails more familiar to the badger, fallow deer and tawny owl than human feet.

I choose my path according to the weather, my schedule, or

mood. On sunny days I tend to head into the hills to drink in
the panoramic views. In the autumn I lose myself on thickly
carpeted forest trails, foraging for puffballs and fairy-ring cham-
pignons. In the summer we light fires at dusk in hidden glades
and sometimes camp wild.

This book is a 'simple guide' to the complex living landscape of prayer. Get your boots on – this isn't going to be a
concrete highway. I realise there are times when we all just
need the fastest possible route to God – when you're skidding
on your bike towards a parked car you need the most direct
communication possible: 'Help!' But there's more to prayer
than asking, and God is not in a hurry. There are ways of
praying that are more like exploring than imploring: wood-
land trails on which to shelter, and places so beautiful you'll
stop and whisper praise. There are secret, intimate places to
camp, and paths that take you to the highlands for a longer
view under a bigger sky. It'll be an effort to climb, but worth
it when you arrive.

Along the way, we're going to discover saints who've made
their homes in particular aspects of this varied landscape. You'll
find their stories throughout this book and others featured as
'Heroes' at the end of most chapters. Some have camped out
in contemplation. Others have built hides in the treetops of
prophetic insight. You will eventually find your own favourite
terrain in your walk with God.

I must warn you, however, that none of these trails leads to
God. That's just not how it works. There's no one superior way
to pray. If you're searching for the Holy Grail, go back to where
you began. But as you set out on the many paths of prayer, the
Lord is going to join you on the journey. (He's putting his boots
on right now.) He's going to walk with you in silence, and talk
with you too. The conversation will ebb and flow. He will tell
you things you never knew, and ask you things you never told.
Occasionally you'll lose your sense of him, but not for long.
Sometimes he will suggest a rest or a particular path, but mostly
he will follow your lead, accompanying you every step of the

way until eventually you come full circle, arriving home, knowing yourself known.

We're taking a map with us, of course: the world's most famous prayer – the Lord's Prayer – given to us by Jesus himself for this very purpose: to 'teach us to pray'. In these old, familiar words we are going to discover nine different paths of prayer: *Stillness, Adoration, Petition, Intercession, Perseverance, Contemplation, Listening, Confession* and *Spiritual Warfare.*

And our journey is going to be paced around an easy, four-step rhythm: P.R.A.Y. – *Pause, Rejoice, Ask, Yield.* I'm not a big fan of acronyms – they smack of science textbooks and over-earnest sermons – but this particular one just *works*, because it's simple, sensible and sneakily profound. Try not to take its four steps as hard-and-fast rules – rungs on a ladder to some Seventh Heaven; they are more like dance-steps: fluid, interactive, and open to creative interpretation. Give P.R.A.Y. a chance and it'll lend your prayer life a light structure and an easy flow, whether you're on your own or praying in a group (although, with children, you may want to swap that tricky word 'Yield' for 'Yes').

* * *

I've been writing this book for the best part of two decades, ever since a couple of important discoveries inadvertently launched the 24–7 Prayer movement. The first was that prayer is actually, surprisingly, pretty much the most important thing in life. And the second discovery was that my friends and I were horribly bad at it. Since that inauspicious start, we've been on an adventure of exploration into this simple, difficult, inevitable thing that beats at the heart of life and faith and culture. The teaching in this book flows, therefore, not so much from libraries, seminaries and polished pulpits, but from the practical discoveries we've made in hundreds of pop-up prayer rooms praying night and day over the last twenty years.

You can read *How to Pray* on its own – it's a stand-alone product – but also as a companion volume to *The Prayer Course,* a free online programme for small groups that uses videos and discussion-starters to apply different aspects of the Lord's Prayer to daily life. As I've indicated, at the end of each chapter, you'll find a 'Hero of Prayer' whose life exemplifies the particular type of prayer we've been studying, and links to two additional online resources available at www.prayercourse.org:

1. **TOOL-SHED: 30 PRACTICAL PRAYER TOOLS** – to help you practise this kind of prayer.

2. **THE PRAYER COURSE VIDEO** – relating to each chapter, including a guide for group discussion.

HOW TO P.R.A.Y.

One day Jesus was praying in a certain place.
When he finished, one of his disciples said to him
'Lord, teach us to pray, just as John taught his disciples.'
(Luke 11:1)

Every pilgrim gets a stone in their shoe eventually. You wake up one morning thinking, 'Is this really all there is to knowing the Creator of 100 billion galaxies?' You read the book of Acts and ask, 'Why isn't it like that any more?' Your world falls apart and you desperately need a miracle. You stare up at the stars and feel things bigger than religious language. You say to yourself, 'If this thing is true there's got to be more power, more mystery, more actual personal experience.' And so finally you turn to God, half-wondering whether you're any more than half-serious and say 'Lord, teach me to pray.' And he replies, 'I thought you'd never ask!'

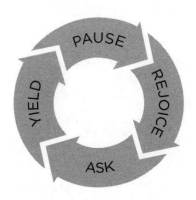

1: Prayer Everywhere

Why pray?

*'One day Jesus was praying
in a certain place . . .'*

---

*More things are wrought by prayer
Than this world dreams of. Wherefore, let thy voice
Rise like a fountain for me night and day.*
(Alfred Lord Tennyson, *Idylls of the King*)[1]

On Mount Athos, two thousand metres above the Aegean Sea, big-bearded Orthodox monks are praying, as they have done for 1,800 years. Thirty miles north of Lagos, more than a million Nigerian Christians are gathering for a monthly prayer meeting at the vast campus of The Redeemed Christian Church of God. On the banks of the River Ganges at Varanasi, Hindu pilgrims are plunging into the sacred waters seeking cleansing and hope. Somewhere in Manhattan a group of addicts on a Twelve Step Programme is meeting, seeking 'through prayer and meditation to improve our conscious contact with God'.[2] High in the Himalayas bells are chiming, strings of coloured prayer flags dancing against sapphire skies. Deep in the forests of Giant Redwood and Douglas Fir on California's Lost Coast, Cistercian nuns are keeping vigil beside the Mattole River, where salmon and steelhead swim.

One person in every four prays the Lord's Prayer each year on Easter Day alone. One person in every six bows towards Mecca up to five times a day. Hasidic Jews stand at Jerusalem's Wailing Wall dressed in black and rocking to and fro like ageing

goths at a silent disco. In front of them, between the giant
stones of Herod's temple, thousands of hand-written prayers
are wedged like badly rolled cigarettes between the bricks.

It's worth pausing at the start of a book like this to acknowledge the unending chorus of human longing: a canticle of sighs
and cries and chiming bells, mutterings in maternity wards,
celestial oratorios and scribbled graffiti. In the words of Rabbi
Heschel, 'Prayer is our humble answer to the inconceivable
surprise of living.'[3]

Native language

Our English word 'prayer' derives from the Latin '*precarius*'. We
pray because life is precarious. We pray because life is marvel-
lous. We pray because we find ourselves lost for many things,
but not for the simplest words like 'please', 'thank you', 'wow',
and 'help'. I prayed when I held our babies for the first time.
I prayed when work overwhelmed me and I knew I couldn't
cope. I prayed when my wife was wheeled away down the
hospital corridor unconscious. I prayed the night I saw the
Northern Lights.

The Canadian psychologist David G. Benner describes prayer
as 'the soul's native language', observing that 'our natural posture
is attentive openness to the divine'.[4] We see this posture in
many great men and women not necessarily known for their
religious devotion. For instance, Abraham Lincoln admitted, 'I
have been driven upon my knees many times by the overwhelming conviction that I had nowhere else to go. My own
wisdom . . . seemed insufficient for that day.'[5]

The entrepreneur Conrad Hilton, founder of the eponymous
hotel chain, surprisingly devotes the last section of his autobi-
ography to the matter of prayer. 'In the circle of successful
living,' he explains, 'prayer is the hub that holds the wheel
together.'[6]

In her semi-autobiographical novel *One True Thing*, Anna
Quindlen depicts the agony of being nineteen years old and
watching her mother receive chemotherapy 'drop by drop by

please-let-it-work-God drop. Oh yes, I prayed in that cubicle, and in the hallway outside, and in the cafeteria,' she says. 'But I prayed to myself without form, only inchoate feelings, one word: please, please, please, please, please.'[7]

The rock-star Dave Grohl admits to praying desperately when his drummer Taylor Hawkins overdosed at England's V Festival. 'I would talk to God out loud as I was walking,' he recalls of the late-night strolls back to Kensington's Royal Garden Hotel from the hospital where his friend lay in a coma. 'I'm not a religious person but I was out of my mind, I was so frightened and heartbroken and confused.'[8]

Elizabeth Gilbert begins her best-selling memoir *Eat, Pray, Love* like this: 'Hello, God. How are you? I'm Liz. It's nice to meet you . . . I've always been a big fan of your work. I haven't ever spoken to you directly before.' And then she starts to cry, 'Can you help me please? I am in desperate need of help. I don't know what to do.' As her tears subside she experiences a peace 'so rare that I didn't want to exhale for fear of scaring it off. I don't know when I'd ever felt such stillness. Then I heard a voice. It was not Charlton Heston, nor was it telling me to build a baseball field. It was my own voice, but a voice I had never heard before.'[9]

My friend Cathy was a militant atheist at the University of Wichita when, late one night in her lodgings, gazing down at her sleeping baby, she was overwhelmed with a desire to give thanks to someone or something for this gift of all gifts. Without a husband or a boyfriend in her life with whom to share her sense of wonder, Cathy whispered a few self-conscious words of gratitude out into the silence and, as she did so, the atmosphere seemed to change. Wave upon wave of love, unlike anything she had ever experienced, came flooding into the room. Kneeling there that night beside her sleeping baby, Cathy relinquished her ardent atheism. More than thirty years later, she remains a follower of Jesus.

The Irish poet Patrick Kavanagh found himself similarly moved to pray by life's unfathomable wonder, an impulse he

describes in his poem 'Canal Bank Walk' as 'the gaping need
of my senses':

> *O unworn world enrapture me, encapture me in a web*
> *Of fabulous grass and eternal voices by a beech,*
> *Feed the gaping need of my senses, give me ad lib*
> *To pray unselfconsciously with overflowing speech,*
> *For this soul needs to be honoured with a new dress woven*
> *From green and blue things and arguments that cannot be*
> *   proven.*[10]

To be human is to pray

From American presidents to Irish poets, and rock stars in
London to single mothers in Wichita, prayer has been 'the
argument that cannot be proven', the 'gaping need' of every
human soul since the very dawn of time. Cave paintings dating
back more than 35,000 years at Maros in Indonesia and Chauvet
in France, were painted, it is thought, as spiritual invocations.
In modern Turkey, the hilltop ruins at Gobekli Tepe are reckoned
to be the remains of a temple 6,000 years older than Britain's
Neolithic Stonehenge, which may itself have been a place of
prayer some 3,000 years before Christ.

And what of the future? Is prayer just the diminishing
shadow of some primitive dawn? Survey after survey answers
'no'.[11] Three hundred years after the Enlightenment the world
is, if anything, becoming more religious, not less.[12] I am based
in England, considered to be one of the more secular nations
in Western Europe, but even here one quarter of those who
describe themselves as 'non-religious' admit that, in fact, they
'take part in some spiritual activity each month, typically
prayer'.[13]

An eminent London surgeon called David Nott illustrates
this apparent contradiction well. He operates in three British
hospitals but chooses to spend his holidays in the world's most
dangerous war zones. 'I am not religious,' he assured Eddie Mair
in a BBC Radio 4 interview:

But every now and again I have to pray and I do pray to
God and I ask him to help me because sometimes I am
suffering badly. It's only now and again that I am able to
turn to the right frequency to talk to him and there is not a
doubt in my mind there is a God. I don't need him every
day. I need him every now and again but when I do need
him he is certainly there.[14]

That interview in its entirety had a profound effect on its
listeners. In fact, the experimental artist Patrick Brill (better
known by his strange pseudonym 'Bob and Roberta Smith') was
so moved by David Nott's testimony that he spent the next four
months transcribing every single word in full, letter by letter,
onto a vast canvas, which was then hung in the central hall of
London's Royal Academy as the centrepiece of its Summer
Exhibition – the most popular annual display of contemporary
art in the country, and the oldest in the world.

From primitive cave paintings to the whitewashed walls of
the Royal Academy, the universal impulse to pray permeates
and pulsates through human anthropology and archaeology,
sociology and psychology. It is no exaggeration to say that to
be human is to pray. The question this begs, therefore, is not
so much *why* we pray, but rather *how* to pray and to *whom*, and
for billions of people today, the answer to such questions is to
be found in the revolutionary life and teaching of Jesus Christ.

The Bible and prayer
Very early in the morning, while it was still dark, Jesus got up, left the
house and went off to a solitary place, where he prayed. (Mark 1:35)

The greatest person who ever lived was pre-eminently a man
of prayer. Before launching out in public ministry, he fasted
for more than a month in the wilderness. Before choosing his
twelve disciples, he prayed all night. When he heard the devastating news that his cousin, John, had been executed, 'he
withdrew by boat privately to a solitary place'.[15] After feeding

the five thousand, he was understandably tired but his response was to climb a mountain to pray.

When the pressures of fame threatened to crush him, Jesus prayed.[16] When he was facing his own death in the Garden of Gethsemane, bleeding with fear and failed by his friends, he prayed.[17] Even during those unimaginable hours of physical and spiritual torment upon the cross, Jesus cried out to the one who had apparently forsaken him.[18]

Jesus prayed and he prayed and he prayed.

But it didn't stop there. After his resurrection, Jesus commanded his disciples to follow his example so that the Church was eventually born, as 'they all joined together constantly in prayer'.[19] And then, as it began to grow exponentially, the apostles continued to follow their Lord's example, resolutely prioritising prayer above the clamour of pressing leadership responsibilities.[20]

It was when Peter 'went up on the roof to pray' in the city of Joppa that he received a shocking vision of non-kosher animals presented as food; an epoch-defining epiphany that would catapult the gospel out from its Jewish cradle into the vast harvest-fields of the Gentile world.[21]

We observe equal prayerfulness in Peter's apostolic counterpart Paul, of whom it is said, immediately after his conversion on the road to Damascus, 'he is praying.'[22] Paul's epistles thereafter bubble and fizz with petition, with spontaneous doxologies, and with passionate exhortations to pray. We are engaged, he reminds the Ephesians, in active warfare against dark spiritual powers (Eph. 6). We are caught up, he tells the Romans, in an intense heavenly prayer meeting (Rom. 8). We are edified, he tells the Corinthians, in truths revealed to us only through prayer (1 Cor. 14).

It would be easy to continue in this vein, because the priority of prayer is there to be found in one way or another on almost every page of the Bible, and in every chapter of church history. It is neither a peripheral theme nor an optional extra for the desperate and the devout. It does not belong to some other time in history, nor to some other type of person more spiritual or disciplined or experienced than you and me. Prayer is nothing at all unless it is a matter of vast and all-consuming importance for each one of us.

'Prayer is more than a lighted candle,' insists the theologian George A. Buttrick. 'It is the contagion of health. It is the pulse of Life.'[23] A real relationship with God means walking with him daily, like Adam and Eve in the Garden of Eden. It means talking with him intimately, like Moses with whom 'The Lord would speak . . . face to face, as one speaks to a friend.'[24] And it means listening attentively to his voice because, as Jesus said, 'My sheep listen to my voice; I know them, and they follow me.'[25]

Finding your places of prayer

We are told that, prior to his giving of the Lord's Prayer, 'Jesus was praying in a certain place'.[26] That's significant. There seem to have been certain places in which he preferred to pray. Elsewhere he advised his disciples, 'When you pray, go into your room, close the door.'[27] The location clearly mattered. And then a little later, on the day of Pentecost, we are told that the Holy Spirit first 'filled the whole house where they were sitting' (Acts 2:2) so that the disciples 'saw what seemed to be tongues of fire' (v. 3) and then, moments later, 'all of them were filled with the Holy Spirit' (v. 4).[28] Isn't that an interesting progression? The Holy Spirit filled the place *before* he filled the people.

The ancient Celtic Christians understood very well that the Holy Spirit can saturate places as well as people, describing such sacred sites evocatively as 'thin places'. Your thin place might simply be a particular chair in your house, a bench in the park, a hallowed half-hour on your daily commute, a regular slot in a 24–7 prayer room,[29] or even time in the sanctuary of your bathroom.

'I urge you, too', writes the spiritual teacher Richard Foster, 'to find a place of focus – a loft, a garden, a spare room, an attic, even a designated chair – somewhere away from the routine of life, out of the path of distractions. Allow this spot to become a sacred "tent of meeting".'[30]

Even when you don't really want to pray, a place of prayer can often make it easier. Merely by showing up, you make a declaration of intent. You say, in effect, 'Lord, I don't want to be here, but I'm here!' This has often been my experience with daily devotions and appointments in 24–7 prayer rooms. I may not always want to be there initially – I often drive to the prayer room grumbling, convinced that I can't spare the time and that 24–7 prayer is the worst idea in world history – but simply by showing up I am making myself available, and these are often the times when God meets me most powerfully. After decades of night-and-day prayer, I have come to believe that 99 per cent of it is just showing up; making the effort to become consciously present to the God who is constantly present to us.

Where's your chair?

An advertising executive became a Christian but said that he was too busy to carve out a daily time of prayer. 'It's easy for you,' he told his new pastor. 'You have all the time in the world, but I can't fit anything else into my life.' Perhaps you feel something similar as you begin this book: 'It's easy for Pete,' you may be thinking. 'He's the 24–7 prayer guy. He writes books and talks to squirrels all day. My life is different – it's manic and stressful!'

But the pastor pushed back with a gentle challenge, 'You know,' he said, 'I've always managed to make time for the things I really value.' That new believer went away and bought himself a really nice rocking chair, set it down in front of a window in his house, and began to get up just twenty minutes earlier each day to sit in it, read the Bible, and pray. As he maintained this simple, daily rhythm, his wife and colleagues began to notice that he was becoming less scattered, more peaceful and kind. That rocking chair was becoming his thin place.

Months turned into years, a daily discipline became a holy habit, and then one morning, as he sat there rocking, the Lord invited him to quit his job, sell the family home and relocate from Chicago to Colorado where a church needed his help. It was a life-changing moment that launched his entire family into a new and remarkably fruitful season of life.

Several years later, that successful executive was diagnosed with a particularly aggressive form of incurable cancer, but he continued to keep his appointments with God each morning in that chair. During his last remaining days he found strength there in prayer for the hardest transition of them all.

The day of the funeral dawned and a friend found his grieving wife gazing at that rocking chair. 'What are you going to do with it now?' he enquired. 'Oh, we're going to pass it down to our children and grandchildren,' she replied without hesitation. 'I love to think of them sitting in it the way my husband did, unburdening their hearts, listening to the Lord, letting him shape and direct their lives.'[31]

Where's *your* chair? For my wife, it's a daily dog-walk and weekly appointments with God in a particular coffee shop. For a teacher in our church, it's her classroom where she shows up half an hour early each day to pray quietly over every single desk. For a student who recently came to know Jesus from a strict Sikh background, it's her car. 'Driving is my sanctuary,' she told me. 'I play worship music really loud and my family can't stop me!' Wherever you find your chair, try to visit it daily. Let it become your thin place, a sacred space that helps you walk and talk with God through the many twists and turns of life.

Lord, teach us to pray

Two thousand years ago, the disciples welcomed Jesus back from his regular time and place of prayer with one of the greatest questions of all time: 'Lord,' one of them said, 'teach us to pray.' His response to that simple, humble request was astonishingly generous. He didn't make them feel small. He didn't say, 'You really ought to know by now.' Instead he gave them the greatest prayer in world history. These were men who would go on to have extraordinary prayer lives. They would intercede until buildings shook. They would spring Peter from a high-security jail by the power of prayer. Their very shadows and handkerchiefs would

sometimes heal the sick. They would receive the kinds of revelations that change cultural paradigms. And most remarkably of
all, they would one day find the grace within themselves to pray
for their torturers at the very point of death.

The disciples were to become mighty prayer warriors, but it
wasn't automatic. Prayer didn't get beamed down upon them
from heaven. It wasn't a guaranteed perk of the apostolic job.
Prayer had to be learned the hard way, and their schooling was
to begin on a particular day with this simple, touchingly vulnerable request: 'Lord, teach us to pray.'

And so, of course, he did.

* * *

In this opening chapter I have sought to set out the historical
and biblical case for prayer and the universal relevance of sacred
space, from the Wailing Wall in Jerusalem to a rocking chair
in Colorado. My intention has been to reassure you that learning
to pray really is the least weird, most natural, necessary and
wonderful thing you can possibly do, and to encourage you to
follow Christ's example in setting apart 'a certain place' (or
certain places) for doing so regularly. In later chapters (3–12)
we will focus on particular dimensions of prayer such as adoration, petition, intercession and contemplation. But first, in the
next chapter, we are going to address the fundamental question
at the heart of this book; how to pray at its simplest, most
literal level.

You can discover more about the aspects of prayer discussed
in this chapter at www.prayercourse.org including:

- **PRAYER TOOL:** *How to Pray the Lord's Prayer.*

- **FURTHER READING:** *Prayer: Finding the Heart's True
  Home,* by Richard Foster.

2: Keeping it Simple

Starting out in prayer

'Lord, teach us to pray . . .'

———————————

The best bit of advice I ever received about how to pray was this: *keep it simple, keep it real, keep it up.* You've got to *keep it simple* so that the most natural thing in the world doesn't become complicated, weird and intense.

You've got to *keep it real* because when life hurts like hell you're going to be tempted to pretend you're fine. And then at other times, when you make a mess of things, you're going to be tempted to hide from God (which never really works) and end up hiding from yourself (which works quite well).

And you've got to *keep it up* because life is tough, the battle is fierce, and God is not an algorithm. The journey of faith demands a certain bloody-mindedness of us all, not least in the realm of prayer.

* * *

It was the holiest moment of my day: bedtime prayers with one of our boys. Hudson was warm and clean, smelling of soap and dressed in his superhero pyjamas. Soon enough he would be asleep. Peace would reign again in our home. All would be well in the world.

'No bad dreams, Lord,' I whispered. 'May Huddy know how much you love him and grow up to be a Christian.'

'No!' a little voice yelled in my ear.

'No, Daddy,' he said again, scowling and indignant. 'I don't *want* to be a Christian when I grow up!'

'Oh,' I said, a little deflated, trying not to look disappointed.
'Do you, um, mind telling me why?'

'When I grow up, Daddy,' he said, puffing out his pigeon
chest, 'I want to be *Batman*.'

'Oh,' I said again, and pulled him a little closer. We sat there
quietly for a bit.

'I think,' I ventured at last, 'it's possible to be both.'

There are definitely days I'd prefer a set of personal superpowers
to slogging away at the slow, confusing business of prayer. God
knows that we don't always find it easy to string a sentence
together in his presence. 'He remembers', as the Psalmist says,
'that we are dust.'[1] He understands that we sometimes get
tongue-tied, distracted, overwhelmed and confused. He doesn't
get insecure if we occasionally doubt his existence. He sees our
bruised and broken hearts and accepts that prayer hasn't always
seemed to help. He isn't in the least bit annoyed that we occasionally find talking to him a bit boring. Or that we would
sometimes prefer to scale the Empire State Building covered
in spandex, than merely, meekly 'go into your room, close the
door and pray to your Father, who is unseen'.[2]

But the thing is this: *he likes us.* A lot.

God wants to spend time with us even more than we want
to spend time with him. This is a mind-blowing truth. It means
that, whenever you make the effort to approach the Lord in
prayer, he's already waiting there for you with a smile. Try to
remember this next time you step into a prayer room or settle
down with a Bible. He's not frowning. He's not looking bored.
He's probably pleased that you've just picked up this book!

In the coming chapters we will explore different aspects of
prayer, but the heart pumping life through it all is love. Lose
that sense of prayer as friendship and there'll be nothing left
but theory and technique. As the Ancient Mariner says in
Coleridge's famous poem, 'He prayeth well, who loveth well.'[3]

In the previous chapter I said that prayer is the most natural
thing in the world because we are created for friendship with

God, but how do we actually do it? How do we *keep it simple*, when prayer can be so confusing and hard? And how are we to *keep it real*, when there's so much hype and hypocrisy in our world and in ourselves? And how are we to *keep it up* when (let's be honest) sometimes we all feel like giving up?

1. Keeping it simple

Jesus warns us quite specifically against getting over-complicated in prayer:

> The world is full of so-called prayer warriors . . . peddling techniques for getting what you want from God. Don't fall for that nonsense. This is your Father you are dealing with, and he knows better than you what you need. With a God like this loving you, you can pray very simply.[4]

He then goes on to give the Lord's Prayer, which was just thirty-one words long in its original language, and also originally rhymed. Jesus wrote us a poem![5] Having advocated simplicity in prayer, he modelled it with a short, rhyming prototype that takes thirty seconds to recite in English and fits in a single tweet. As Archbishop Justin Welby says, the Lord's Prayer is 'simple enough to be memorised by small children, and yet profound enough to sustain a whole lifetime of prayer'.[6]

* * *

If you're new to faith, you will probably have all sorts of sensible questions about prayer. I remember a sophisticated-looking lady coming to speak to me one Sunday after a service. 'I'm new to Christianity,' she said. 'Is it all right if I talk to God in the shower?'

I was driving a friend across town. He was a brand new believer and I suggested we pray. 'No way!' he screamed and tried to grab the wheel, terrified that I was about to close my eyes.

There are very few rules for Christians when it comes to prayer. Yes, of course we can pray in the shower, or while driving our cars. We are not required to close our eyes, to adopt a particular posture, to dress in a certain way, to wash ourselves ritually, or to use a fixed form of words simply to be heard by God. Some of these things can on occasions be helpful, as we shall see later, but the writer of Hebrews is clear that God's presence is freely available to us all at any time, in any place, through Jesus (Hebrews 10:19).

God invites you to pray simply, directly and truthfully in the full and wonderful weirdness of the way he's actually made you. Take a walk in the rain. Write prayers on the soles of your shoes. Sing the Blues. Rap. Write Petrarchan Sonnets. Sit in silence in a forest. Go for a run until you sense God's smile; throw yourself down a water-slide, yelling hallelujah if that's honestly your thing. 'I pray all the time,' said the Native American pastor Richard Twiss, a member of the Sicangu Oyate tribe in South Dakota:

> My prayers are not only talking to God. They are questions, they are dialogue, they are the burning of sage and incense. When I'm dancing in the pow-wow, every step is a prayer: I dance my prayers for the people. Sometimes I imagine my prayers, I fantasize my prayers; they're not always audible.[7]

2. Keeping it real

When you pray, do not keep on babbling like pagans, for they think they will be heard because of their many words. Do not be like them, for your Father knows what you need before you ask him. (Matt. 6:7–8)

Jesus invites us to keep prayer simple, and also to keep it real. On one occasion, he told a surprising story about two men arriving at the temple to pray. One of them, a Pharisee, stood and spoke with confidence, ticking all the right religious boxes with his high-profile fasting and tithing. But the other man, a despised tax collector, 'would not even look up to heaven' but

hid in the shadows muttering, 'God, have mercy on me, a sinner.'
'I tell you,' concluded Jesus, and I imagine him eye-balling the
Pharisees in the crowd as he did so, 'this man – the tax collector,
rather than the other – went home justified by God.'[8] As the
Trappist monk Thomas Merton says: 'God is far too real to be
met anywhere other than in reality.'[9]

The author Anne Lamott wrote a refreshingly irreverent book
about prayer with a title I've always liked: *Help, Thanks, Wow.*
These three words, she argues, are the only prayers we will ever
need. Whether or not we agree, she does a brilliant job driving
home the need for radical honesty in prayer.

> My belief is that, when you are telling the truth you are close
> to God. If you say to God 'I am exhausted and depressed
> beyond words, and I don't like You at all right now, and I
> recoil from most people who believe in You,' that might be
> the most honest thing you've ever said. If you told me you
> had said to God, 'It is all hopeless, and I don't have a clue if
> You exist, but I could use a hand,' it would almost bring tears
> to my eyes, tears of pride in you, for the courage it takes to
> get real – really real.[10]

Picking a fight with God

One dark night, when my wife, Sammy, was in hospital awaiting
brain surgery and long before we knew for sure that she was
going to survive, my friend Dan kindly came to pray with me.

'Lord, if this is your time to take Sammy home,' Dan ventured
at last, articulating my deepest dread, 'would you please give
Pete strength to bear the unbearable?' It can't have been an
easy thing to pray. It was a faithful and biblical thing to ask,
but I was having none of it. 'No deal,' I said, interrupting without
apology. 'No way, God. Over my dead body!' I was out of my
chair, pacing the room. 'If you're planning to take my wife from
me, if you're planning to take a mum from her two little boys,
well, you're going to have to fight me for her.'

Dan looked nervous but I didn't care.

'And you're going to have to find someone else to do your PR in future too,' I continued. 'I resign. I quit. I'm not going around telling people you're good if you don't prove it to me now.' Tears were streaming down my cheeks. 'God, I just don't care what *your* will is. Let me tell you what *my* will is – I want my wife to live. I want our boys to know their mum. And if her name is up there on some celestial wall-planner, if she's destined to die of this thing, then what I want, what I *need*, is for you to sort it out.'

I was almost howling my pain while poor Dan just sat there, probably wondering whether it was OK to say 'Amen' to this kind of irreverence.

It was one of the most honest prayers I'd ever prayed. For a while I was embarrassed about the way I'd tried to pick a fight that night with God, ashamed that I hadn't been trusting enough, or holy enough, to echo the magnificent submission of Jesus in his darkest hour: 'not my will but yours be done'.

But then, one day, the Lord showed me very gently that in fact he had cherished my willingness to fight for Sammy's life because he loves her too. That he wouldn't have expected me to do anything less. That he himself had begged the Father 'take this cup from me', before he managed the other bit.

Honest to God

The Bible is often way more honest than the Church. You've probably noticed how many of the Psalms (the Jewish prayer book) are not happy-clappy but cries of unresolved pain. Only this morning I read a great example as part of my regular prayer time: 'Evening and morning and at noon, I will complain and murmur. And he will hear my voice' (55:17, NASB). That's a lot of complaining and murmuring!

One of the Bible's greatest patriarchs, Jacob, wrestled with God in a night of prayer so violent that he was wounded – never healed – for the rest of his life.

Moses whined about the very people God had called him to lead: 'Why are you treating me this way? What did I ever do to you to deserve this? Did I conceive them? Was I their mother? So why dump the responsibility of this people on me?'[11]

The prophet Jeremiah ranted – there's no other word for it – at God: 'You deceived me, LORD, and I was deceived; you overpowered me and prevailed. I am ridiculed all day long; everyone mocks me.'[12]

The truly remarkable thing about all the rude, irreverent, self-pitying prayers recorded in the Bible is not that they were prayed in the first place, but that they were never redacted from the text. These outrageous prayers were prayed by a litany of anti-heroes – capable of arch narcissism, crass stupidity, and the very heights of nobility too. A bit like you and me.

> What seem our worst prayers may really be, in God's eyes, our best. Those which are least supported by devotional feeling . . . these may come from a deeper level than feeling. God sometimes seems to speak to us most intimately when he catches us, as it were, off our guard. (C.S. Lewis)[13]

3. Keeping it up
Jesus told his disciples a parable to show them that they should always pray and not give up. (Luke 18:1)

No matter how simply and honestly we pray, it's easy to lose heart and tempting to give up when our prayers don't seem to be working. That's why it's not enough just to *keep it simple* and *keep it real*. Jesus also says that we must 'always pray and not give up'. This is such an important consideration for every single one of us that an entire chapter of this book is devoted to dealing with the disappointments of delayed and unanswered prayer. But for now, let's just acknowledge that prayer can be a lot like stacking dominoes. We pray the same thing we've prayed one hundred times before until suddenly the whole lot comes down. The breakthrough occurs. The miracle happens. It's not that we finally found the right formula. It's simply that we didn't give up praying one prayer too soon.

The pioneering missionary educationalist, Frank Laubach, whose literacy programmes taught more than sixty million people to read, compared praying to throwing rocks in a swamp. Each rock sinks without trace. The exercise seems pointless. But keep going long enough, keep throwing those rocks, and the swamp will eventually be filled. One day a rock will be thrown that will not sink. Solid ground will begin to appear.

I've found that one of the most important keys to 'keeping it up' in prayer – throwing those rocks into the swamp – is to develop the discipline of a daily 'quiet time'. Jesus once invited his friends, 'Come with me by yourselves to a quiet place and get some rest',[14] and millions of his followers ever since have allocated a little time each day to retreat with Jesus to a quiet place. For prayer and Bible reading see Tool-shed: *How to Have a Quiet Time* (prayercourse.org).

As someone who struggles with all kinds of self-discipline – attending the gym, declining the chocolate cake, going to bed before midnight, bothering to floss my teeth and, yes, even maintaining regular times of prayer – I hesitate to advocate the rigidity of any such routine. I don't want to put anything heavy or unsustainable on you as you seek to grow in prayer. But here is the great and inescapable truth, taught in Scripture, modelled by Christ and advocated without exception by all the heroes of our faith: you cannot grow in prayer without some measure of effort and discomfort, self-discipline and self-denial. Just as you cannot get physically fit without regular exercise and a healthy diet, so your spiritual growth will be determined, to a very significant extent, by the prayer exercises you choose (or do not choose) to establish and sustain.

The architecture of romance
When Sammy and I first fell in love we were embarrassingly obsessed with each other. We would talk for hours on the phone and wanted to spend every waking moment in one another's company. The mention of Sammy's name could make my heart

skip a beat. We never had to plan date nights because we were together most of the time.

But we have now been married for a quarter of a century and let's just say it's no longer quite so intense! If the mention of Sammy's name was still making my heart leap, I'd probably be dead. Without the discipline of scheduled 'date nights' we could quite easily go weeks on end without talking properly or investing into any form of romance.

DELIGHT WITHOUT DISCIPLINE EVENTUALLY DISSIPATES

I'm sure that some young loved-up couples might look at us these days and think, 'We must never become like Pete and Sammy. Let's make sure that our relationship is always wild and spontaneous. Let's never get to the place where we become so boring and predictable that we have to resort to scheduling romance!'

But here's the thing: Sammy and I have a relationship today, after twenty-five years, that is more fulfilling than anything we could have understood back in those first days of furious infatuation. And it has been the discipline of daily communication, of frequent date nights, of apologising regularly and renewing our vows annually, that has kept our love alive. No one is designed to live at a peak of emotional intensity for years on end. It wouldn't be healthy. It wouldn't be sustainable or real. Delight without discipline eventually, inevitably dissipates. It runs out of steam. But when delight and discipline learn to dance, relationships thrive. They mature and endure. Sammy and I may no longer be that young, loved-up couple, leaking pheromones like diesel fumes, but, thanks to the holy habits we have maintained together over many years, we are now a quarter of a century closer to becoming that crinkly old couple walking hand in hand down the street, somehow still in love.

Just as an enduring marriage must be built upon consistent rhythms and routines, so too our relationship with God survives and thrives only through disciplines such as Bible study, fellowship, confession and prayer, Otherwise, says the Bible translator Eugene Peterson, 'we are at the mercy of glands and weather and indigestion. And there is no mercy in any of them.'[15] A Christian who prays only when they feel like it may survive but they will never thrive. Their vast, innate potential will be stunted because grace needs a little space to take root between the cracks of a person's life.

If anyone ever had an excuse *not* to pray in any kind of regimented way, it was surely the sinless Son of God. Jesus could so easily have argued (as some do today), 'Look, everything I do is basically prayer. My life is a continual conversation with the Father. When I sleep, when I drink a cup of water, it is prayer. I don't need special times and places. I don't need to be restricted by rules.' But read the Gospels and you'll see that Jesus prayed diligently, continually making time to be alone with his Father.

Making it easy and enjoyable
Many people prefer to pray at the start of the day, as Jesus often did: 'Very early in the morning, while it was still dark, Jesus got up, left the house and went off to a solitary place, where he prayed.'[16] Others find mornings difficult and set aside time at night before bed. Jesus did this too: 'Each evening he went out to spend the night on the hill called the Mount of Olives.'[17] Commuters often deploy half an hour in the car or on a train to pray and absorb God's word. Busy mothers of young children may find it easiest to snatch bite-sized moments during the day. Susanna Wesley, the mother of both John and Charles (and the 'Hero of Simple Prayer' profiled at the end of this chapter), would pull her apron over her head, and whenever she did this, her ten children (yes, ten) knew that she was praying and not to be disturbed.

Whatever time of day works best for you, the key to turning a sporadic and spontaneous approach to prayer into a sustainable, transformational routine is to make it as *easy* and *enjoyable* as you can.

- *Making it easy.* Deciding to rise before dawn for an hour of unbroken intercession every day for the rest of your life is unlikely to prove sustainable. Much better to set yourself an achievable target, aiming initially for perhaps just fifteen minutes a day at a convenient time in a conducive place. You will be pleasantly surprised at how easy this is, and how often your quiet time overruns. What's more, if you keep it up for two months straight, psychologists say that it could become a lifelong habit.[18]
- *Making it enjoyable.* It's also important to make your daily devotions as *enjoyable* as possible. Most days I look forward to my moments of quiet, alone with the Lord, clutching a big mug of coffee in the morning, pausing to pray the Lord's Prayer at noon, and then strolling out under the stars at night. There is an excitement about opening my Bible thinking, 'I wonder what the Lord is going to say to me today?' It's a privilege to be able to discuss my concerns with the living God.

People often ask what my personal prayer rhythm looks like. I hesitate to share something so private, but have decided to do so in the simple hope that it can help others develop their own easy, enjoyable patterns of prayer, but there are two provisos. First, please don't feel you need to copy my routine. My circumstances and preferences may well be entirely different to your own. Second, you must understand that I often fail. Life frequently gets busy and I am easily distracted. But when this happens I try not to beat myself up. I don't feel any less loved or called or useful to the Lord. I simply pick myself up and start again.

I generally eat three square meals a day and try, in a similar way, to feed myself spiritually three times a day: in the morning, at midday and last thing at night:

- *Morning: quiet time.* Almost every morning I start my day
  with a little time of Bible reading and prayer. I alternate
  seasonally between various trusted devotional frameworks
  including Nicky Gumbel's *Bible in One Year*, the
  Northumbria Community's *Celtic Daily Prayer*, and Phyllis
  Tickle's *Divine Hours*.[19] (For advice on how to develop your
  own daily quiet time, see the end of this chapter.)
- *Midday: Lord's Prayer.* At noon each day an alarm on my
  phone reminds me to pause and pray the Lord's Prayer.
  This is something I do quite quickly (and silently when I'm
  in a public place), but sometimes I am able to pray it more
  slowly, personalising and exploring each line. (See Tool-
  shed: *How to Pray the Lord's Prayer.*)
- *Night: Examen.* Before heading to bed, I will often sit
  quietly or take the dogs out for a short walk in order to
  process the day using my own version of an old Ignatian
  prayer tool called the *Examen* (see Chapter 10). In these
  moments, I do not rant or rave. I don't make big requests. I
  hush my soul, remembering the day with gratitude and
  preparing my soul to sleep.

Between these three fixed points, there are other ways in which
I weave prayer into the fabric of my ordinary life. For instance,
at the gym three mornings a week, while huffing and puffing
on the cross trainer, I endeavour to exercise my soul as well as
my body by listening to worship music, Bible teaching or interesting podcasts. At dinner-time it has become a family ritual
to spin our big, clunky landline phone on the table. Whoever
it points towards – non-Christian guests included – is granted
two great privileges: to say grace, giving thanks to God for the
meal we are about to enjoy, and to ask any question at all of
every single person around the table. Over the years, we've
faced every kind of inquisition. Most embarrassing experience?
Earliest memory? Worst thing you've ever eaten? Naughtiest
thing you've ever done? It's a delightful discipline that draws
everyone into the sacraments of fellowship and thanksgiving.

These, then, are the easy, enjoyable routines that punctuate my day with a greater conversational awareness of God's presence. If you were a fly on the wall, I think you would be unimpressed by how simple and short many of my prayer times can be, how often I forget one or other of them, the trivia I mostly discuss with the Lord, and how frequently I have to whisper, 'Oh Lord, I'm so sorry.'

* * *

In this chapter I have set out three of the most basic building blocks in the Christian approach to prayer: simplicity, honesty and perseverance. I have also encouraged you to establish your own easy, enjoyable prayer routine, such as a daily quiet time.

But finding space and time to pray may not be your biggest challenge. You may already pray quite regularly but be finding it a little dry, and you're longing for a bit more depth. So let's take the first surprising step of the P.R.A.Y. process: It's one of the most counter-intuitive, counter-cultural, easily ignored keys to a deeper, more fulfilling prayer life that to start we must stop. To move forward in prayer we must first learn to 'Pause'!

MORE ON SIMPLE PRAYER:

- **PRAYER COURSE SESSION**: #1: Why Pray?

- **PRAYER TOOLS**: (1) How to Have a Quiet Time (2) How to Pray the *Examen* (prayercourse.org).

- **FURTHER READING**: *Sacred Pathways*, by Gary Thomas.

HERO OF SIMPLE PRAYER:

Susanna Wesley:
Mother of Methodism

The health of Susanna Wesley, who was known as the 'Mother of Methodism', was poor, her marriage to a penniless preacher was deeply dysfunctional, she lost nine children in infancy and raised ten more almost single-handedly. Their home was burned down. Twice. Her husband was imprisoned. Twice. And yet her simple, honest, persevering prayers undoubtedly changed the world.

Susanna Wesley proved herself to be a formidable leader long before her sons John and Charles rose to fame. When her husband, the Rector of Epworth parish church, was imprisoned for financial mismanagement and his replacement in the pulpit failed miserably to preach the gospel, Susanna took matters into her own hands. She launched a Sunday school in the kitchen for her children, but it began to attract so many of their neighbours that the meeting was quickly reconvened in the barn. Before long, 200 people were gathering every Sunday to listen to Susanna reading sermons, to sing Psalms and to pray. Meanwhile, the church building nearby languished almost empty.

Susanna gave her children six hours of schooling a day, educating her daughters the same as her sons, plus an additional hour a week of undivided attention with each one of them. How on earth did she do all this? How did she survive the loss of nine children, and the heartbreak of a volatile marriage, without becoming broken and bitter? And how did she manage such a frenetic household, while also establishing a Sunday school and educating ten children, two of whom would rise to the heights of international influence?

Susanna Wesley was pre-eminently a woman of prayer. It was as she waited upon the Lord each day that her strength was renewed again and again.[20]

But none of this was easy. There was nowhere at home she could hide away to pray, so whenever Susanna wanted time with the Lord she would pull her apron over her head. This was her prayer room and her children knew that she was not to be disturbed. In this way, she would pour her heart out to God, mourning her lost babies, interceding for her infuriating husband, and praying for each of her children by name. Such simple, maternal prayers, whispered daily beneath an apron, could hardly have been answered more powerfully.

Susanna Wesley exemplifies the world-changing power of simple, persevering prayer. Finding herself called to make disciples, not of distant nations but of her own little tribe at home, she applied herself to the task tirelessly. And by praying faithfully for those ten children, Susanna Wesley, a housewife with a hard life from a small town in rural England, became the mother of some eighty million Methodists in more than 130 nations today.

A prayer of Susanna Wesley

Help me, Lord, to remember that religion is not to be confined to the church, or closet, nor exercised only in prayer and meditation, but that everywhere I am in Your presence. So may my every word and action have a moral content. May all the happenings of my life prove useful and beneficial to me. May all things instruct me and afford me an opportunity of exercising some virtue and daily learning and growing toward Your likeness. Amen.

STEP 1: PAUSE
Slowing & Centring

Be still and know that I am God.
(Ps. 46:10)

To start we must stop. To move forward we must pause. This is the first step in a deeper prayer life: put down your wish-list and wait. Sit quietly. Be still. Become fully present in place and time so that your scattered senses can re-centre themselves on God's eternal presence. Stillness and silence prepare your mind and prime your heart to pray from a place of greater peace, faith and adoration. In fact, it is in itself an important form of prayer.

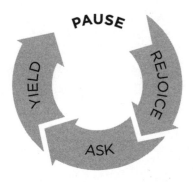

3: Slowing & Centring

How to be still before God

All of humanity's problems stem from man's
inability to sit quietly in a room alone.
(Blaise Pascal, *Pensées*)[1]

The human soul is wild and shy. The Psalmist compares it to a deer panting for streams of water.[2] Celtic folklore depicted it as a stag, noble and coy. It hides away from the noise of life, refuses to come on command like some slavering, domesticated pet. But when we are still, it emerges, inquisitive and quiveringly alive.

In prayer, as in life, 'there is a time to be silent, and a time to speak' (Eccl. 3:7). If we want to get better at hearing the One who speaks 'in a still, small voice', we must befriend silence.[3] If we are to host the presence of the One who says, 'Be still, and know that I am God', we must ourselves become more present.[4] We expect his voice to boom like thunder, but mostly he whispers. We expect him to wear hobnail boots, but he tiptoes and hides in the crowd. We expect him to be strange, but he 'comes to us disguised as our life'.[5]

The best way to start praying, therefore, is actually to stop praying. To pause. To be still. To put down your prayer list and surrender your own personal agenda. To stop talking *at* God long enough to focus on the wonder of who he actually is. To 'be still before the Lord and wait patiently for him'.[6]

* * *

When our sons were quite little I would sometimes walk through the door after several days away, only to be greeted by one of them yelling, 'Dad, have you got anything *nice* for me?' or 'Dad, my brother's not *sharing*', or even, 'Dad, what's for dinner?'

'Well, I'm so glad you've missed me!' I would call upstairs. 'Any chance of a hug down here?' I wanted them to acknowledge my presence properly before bombarding me with requests. To look me in the eyes and say very simply, 'Welcome home, Daddy!'

In a way, this is what Jesus models in the opening lines of the Lord's Prayer. Before we launch into a long list of all the stuff we need – daily bread, forgiveness of sins, deliverance from evil – he tells us to pause, to address God affectionately as 'Our Father', and respectfully, 'hallowed be your name'.

Prayer can easily become a frenetic extension of the manic way I live too much of my life. Distracted and driven, I step into the courts of the King without modulation, without introduction, without slowing my pace or lifting my face to meet his gaze. But the sages teach us that true prayer is not so much something we say, nor is it something we do; it is something we *become*. It is not transactional but relational. And it begins, therefore, with an appropriate awareness of the One to whom we come.

The parable of the deranged greyhound and the wild, dog-eating chair

The tranquillity of Guildford's picturesque cobbled High Street was shattered one sunny morning by the yelping of a dog and a strange metallic clattering.

Suddenly, a crazed greyhound came scrabbling around the corner with its whippet tail between its wild legs, weaving between shouting shoppers, frantic with fear and hotly pursued by one of those cheap chrome bistro chairs. The chair, which was attached to the other end of the dog's lead, seemed alive, like a dancing snake weaving and flailing, striking and biting at that terrified animal's rear.

Perhaps the dog's owner was still inside, unaware of his pet's plight, innocently queuing for coffee. A movement must have made that chair twitch, which had made the dog jump, which had made the chair leap, which had made the dog scamper, which had made the chair pounce, which had made the dog yelp, which had made shoppers shout, which had made the dog run even more frantically, pursued all the while by this terrifying piece of metal and these crowds of screaming, grabbing strangers. The faster it ran, the wilder the chair's pursuit, the higher it bounced, the harder it pounced, the louder it banged and clanged and zinged on the cobbles. For all I know, that dog is running still.

We can all live our lives a lot like that demented greyhound. Driven and disorientated by irrational fears, pursued by entire packs of bloodthirsty bistro chairs, too scared to simply stop. And so God speaks firmly into the cacophony of human activity. The Master commands the creature to 'Sit!' Jesus rebukes the storm. 'He *makes* me lie down', as the famous Psalm puts it. And, of course, we find it intensely difficult to obey, but as we do so, perspective is restored. Terrors turn back into bistro chairs.

Why is it that so many people today find themselves drawn to the simplicity of marathon running, long-distance cycling, fishing (still Britain's most popular pastime), the practice of mindfulness, yoga and the cult of 'de-cluttering' (ironically now all multimillion-dollar industries)? Why do we binge mindlessly on Netflix at night, and gaze – like monks before icons – at our smartphones on the 07:34 to Waterloo? We seem to be increasingly attracted to activities that put the world's relentless demands on hold, forcing us to focus for a few eternal moments on a single, simple thing. Hot yoga? Tetris? A lakeside in the pouring rain? Anything to assuage those pesky bistro chairs.

God understands our deep need for stillness, order and freedom from ultimate responsibility, because he has designed us to live humbly, seasonally and at peace. He himself rested and established the Sabbath, inviting each one of us to press pause regularly, saying, 'Be still, and know that I am God.'⁷ The Latin for being still here is *'vacate'* – the very word we use to describe vacating a place or taking a vacation. In other words, God is inviting us 'to take a holiday, to be leisurely or free', because this is the context in which his presence is known. Perhaps we might paraphrase this verse: 'Why don't you take a vacation from being god, and let me be God instead for a change?'

YOU MUST SEEK SOLITUDE AND SILENCE AS IF YOUR LIFE DEPENDS ON IT, BECAUSE IN A WAY IT DOES

Eugene Peterson says that 'Life's basic decision is rarely, if ever, whether to believe in God or not, but whether to worship or compete with him.'⁸ One of the main differences between you and God is that God doesn't think he's you! Moments of stillness at the start of a prayer time are moments of surrender in which we stop competing with God, relinquish our messiah complexes and resign from trying to save the planet. We stop expecting everyone and everything else to orbit our preferences; we re-centre our priorities on the Lord and acknowledge, with a sigh of relief, that he is in control and we are not. Much to our surprise, the world keeps turning quite well without our help. Slowly, our scattered thoughts start to become more centred. Bistro chairs finally settle down.

Selah

The word *selah* appears seventy-one times in the Psalms – the Hebrew prayer book. It may have been a technical note to the people reciting the Psalm, or to the musicians playing it, but no one really knows for sure what it originally meant or why it is there. Our best guess is that it was an instruction to 'pause' and an invitation to 'weigh' the meaning of the words we are praying.

Whenever possible, I try to *selah* at the start of a prayer time by sitting (or sometimes walking) silently for a few minutes without saying or doing anything at all. It's preferable to do this in a serene environment, of course, but equally possible to find stillness on a crowded train, at a desk in a noisy office, or even hidden in that modern-day hermitage: a toilet cubicle. Stopping to be still before we launch into prayer helps us to re-centre our scattered thoughts, priming our hearts and minds to worship.

If you have a smart phone, it's a good idea at this point to switch it to flight-mode, not just to prevent interruptions, but also to train your brain to switch off from the abstractions and distractions of life, to become more fully present whenever and wherever you turn to God in prayer.

Pausing before you pray may sound simple – barely worthy of its own chapter – but it is rarely easy. Invariably my mind rebels against any kind of stillness. The greyhound keeps running. The temptation to rush headlong into my prayer list is almost irresistible. A tyranny of demands and distractions strikes up in the unfamiliar silence like a brass band parading around my skull. One Augustinian monk describes it memorably as that 'inner chaos going on in our heads, like some wild cocktail party of which we find ourselves the embarrassed host'.[9]

I cannot emphasise too strongly how important it is for your spiritual, mental and physical wellbeing that you learn to silence the world's relentless chatter for a few minutes each day, to become still in the depths of your soul. You must seek solitude and silence as if your life depends on it, because in a way it does. When you are stressed, your adrenal glands release the hormone cortisol, which impairs your capacity for clear thinking and healthy decision-making. But as you sit quietly, the cortisol subsides and things become clearer. The swirling sediment of life settles down quite quickly. You become more aware of your own presence in place and time, and of God's gentle, subsuming presence around and within you too.

Stilling the house

Five hundred years ago, St John of the Cross captured the tranquillity of such moments in a lovely phrase: 'my house now being all stilled'. The lights are off, doors locked, the street outside has fallen silent and inside every living thing has been put to bed. Finally, I am ready to host the whispering King.

Sometimes, having stilled my house, I spend my entire prayer time in silence, simply enjoying God's presence without saying or doing anything. I used to worry that this wasn't real prayer – that I had somehow wasted my time – but I have come to understand that these can be some of the most beautiful times of communion. 'I have calmed and quietened myself, I am like a weaned child with its mother', as the Psalmist says. 'Like a weaned child, I am content.'[10] In such moments, language becomes unnecessary and even inappropriate. Time stops and words retire. It is enough just to be together like close friends sitting in comfortable silence, without needing to fill the space with a fusillade of speech. In the words of Anthony of the Desert more than sixteen centuries ago: 'Perfect prayer is not to know that you are praying.'[11]

Centring prayer

There are several simple practices that can help you to centre your scattered senses as you prepare to pray. It may be helpful to think of them in four steps:

1. *Relax.* Start off by sitting comfortably without doing anything for a few moments, perhaps with your palms open in your lap. Take note of the places in your body where you are holding tension, and deliberately relax in each one. Your posture matters. The Bible describes kneeling, raising hands, lying prostrate, even dancing. Try to find a posture in prayer that is both comfortable and meaningful as you approach the Lord.

2. *Breathe.* As you relax, take deep, slow breaths, inhaling the life-breath of the Holy Spirit and exhaling your concerns with leisurely sighs. A common symptom of anxiety and other forms of stress can be shallow and erratic breathing patterns, which reduce the oxygen levels in our brains, exacerbating the very agitation that triggered our shallow breathing in the first place. Breathing deeply reverses this vicious cycle, helping us to think more clearly, slowing our hearts, reducing our cortisol levels, and calming our mental chatter. Some people get a bit jumpy about this kind of thing. They worry that breathing techniques might be the gateway to Eastern mysticism or New Age deception. Nothing could be further from the truth if our focus is Jesus. When he appeared to his disciples after his resurrection 'he breathed on them and said, "Receive the Holy Spirit."'[12] As one of the primary biblical metaphors for the Holy Spirit, and one of the primary biological markers of life itself, breathing has belonged to the lexicon of legitimate Judeo-Christian spirituality from the very beginning when God created Adam by 'breathing into his nostrils the breath of life'.[13] What could be less sinister, more sensible and universal than simply breathing well in order to function well?

3. *Speak.* As you sit quietly and breathe slowly, you may also find it helpful to repeat a prayer word or phrase, in time with your breathing. You could say 'Father in heaven' while breathing in, and 'hallowed be your name' while breathing out. Some people adopt the famous *Jesus Prayer*, which dates back to the great saints of the Egyptian Desert in the fifth century: 'Lord Jesus Christ, Son of God, have mercy on me, a sinner.' Traditions even older than the Desert Fathers advocate the prayerful repetition of the Aramaic word '*maranatha*', drawn from 1 Corinthians 16:22, which means 'Come, Lord' or 'the Lord has come'. Francis of Assisi's centring prayer was equally simple: 'My God and my all'. His followers to this day repeat this phrase, again and again, as a means of prayerful adoration, meditation and

surrender. Even more simply, I often begin my prayer times
by whispering 'Thank you, Jesus', or by speaking in tongues
because, as St Paul says, 'Anyone who speaks in a tongue
edifies themselves'.[14] (See Tool-shed: *How to Pray in
Tongues*.) Whatever language and phrase you choose, the
point is not to think too earnestly about the words themselves but rather to use them as a way of displacing
distractions, focusing your mind on the present moment
and the presence of God within it.

4. *Repeat*. When distractions come, as they inevitably will,
   don't worry. Simply return to the process of relaxing,
   breathing, and repeating your prayer phrase until stillness
   resumes. The compass needle will soon return to magnetic
   north. There isn't a spiritual giant who didn't sometimes
   struggle to stay focused in prayer. In 1621, the poet John
   Donne, who was also Dean of St Paul's Cathedral, confessed,
   'I invite God and his angels thither, and when they are there,
   I neglect God and his angels for the noise of a fly, for the
   rattling of a coach, for the whining of a door.'[15] When you
   get distracted, you may find it helpful to imagine yourself in
   a rowing boat on a lake. A speedboat has roared by, rocking
   you violently, disrupting the peace. But remain calm. Allow
   your thoughts to settle, and serenity will soon return.[16]

Kinetic centring

Occasionally, none of this works! Sometimes I am too wound
up to find inner stillness in any of these sedentary ways. When
this happens I will instead use physical exercise to burn off a
little adrenaline and calm my mind. It's a shame that so few
of the experts on prayer have ever acknowledged the importance
of movement and exercise for those of us who are active learners
and external processors (at least 50 per cent of the population).
In fact, most of the classic texts on prayer go to great lengths
to advocate the exact opposite; describing in detail how to
sedate our bodies and shut out all external, physical distractions
in order to centre our senses on Christ.

I used to worry that there was something wrong with me because I found it nigh on impossible to be still, to switch off my brain and sit in silence for any length of time without getting distracted or falling asleep. I would often find myself pacing around prayer rooms talking out loud. I seemed to prefer to draw a picture, however badly, than to imagine one. I often wanted to pray aloud, not in my head, and with other people, not on my own. This embarrassing inability to achieve something as straightforward as sitting still and doing nothing for more than a few minutes made me feel unspiritual, doomed to be bad at prayer, certain that I was missing out on some higher echelon of divine encounter.

EXERCISE CAN BE MORE EFFECTIVE THAN SITTING STILL AS A WAY OF CALMING THE BRAIN, DIFFUSING STRESS AND STIMULATING CLARITY OF THOUGHT

But then a school teacher mentioned that many of his pupils processed information kinetically: by *doing* things actively rather than sitting at a desk passively. I met athletes who said they found it easier to encounter God while cycling or running or swimming rather than sitting still with their eyes closed and their hands together the way they had been taught at Sunday school. I met artists who wanted to paint, and sculpt and carve their prayers, dancers who needed to move, and musicians who chose to drum or rap their prayers.

I began to realise that serenity does not always have to be silent, cerebral, solitary or even static. Stillness can be active. In fact, recent medical research has discovered that exercise can be more effective than sitting still as a way of calming the brain, diffusing stress and stimulating clarity of thought. I am not saying that stillness is unimportant – it is vital, as we have seen. But as your heart pressure increases in the first twenty minutes of exercise, a protein called BDNF[17] is released to repair your memory neurons, while the activity in your brain increases to improve concentration, and endorphins trigger a sense of calm and even euphoria. It seems to me that such physiological effects can be gifts of God just as much as other more conventional contemplative approaches.

We know that Jesus himself often prayed actively. On one occasion, he drew in the sand.[18] In the Garden of Gethsemane he threw himself on the ground.[19] He clearly loved to climb and I simply don't believe that Jesus hiked up so many hills early in the morning and late at night merely to get a nice view and a little peace and quiet. I'm convinced that he prayed as he walked, sometimes, no doubt, with sweat on his brow, his lungs panting and his heart pounding. It's an extraordinary thought that, as he hiked the heights of Galilee, BDNF was sharpening the mind of Christ, endorphins were mingling with the blood of Christ, and exercise was enhancing the communion of Christ with his Father.

* * *

In this chapter we have studied the importance of pausing (passively or actively) at the start of a prayer time, in order to still our souls and focus on the Lord. By doing this, even just for a few minutes each day, we re-centre ourselves on Christ's eternal presence, which enables us to pray from a much deeper place of peace, faith and reduced anxiety.

But you may well be thinking, 'OK, fine, I've found a place to pray (Chapter 1), I'm setting aside time to pray (Chapter 2), and I'm even learning to be still (Chapter 3). But what happens now? What do I actually say when I finally find myself alone with the Creator of the cosmos?'

It's time to step beyond the preliminaries of Luke 11:1 and to plunge into the actual words of the Lord's Prayer (Luke 11:2–4). This is where 'how to pray' gets less general, a lot more specific as we take the second step in our P.R.A.Y. process: 'Rejoice!'

A Prayer of Stillness: Psalm 131:1–2

My heart is not proud, Lord, my eyes are not haughty;

I do not concern myself with great matters or things too

wonderful for me.

But I have calmed and quietened myself,

I am like a weaned child with its mother; like a weaned

child I am content.

MORE ON SLOWING & CENTRING:

- **PRAYER TOOLS**: Breath Prayer (prayercourse.org).
- **FURTHER READING**: *Opening to God: Lectio Divina and Life as Prayer*, by David G. Benner.

HEROES OF SLOWING & CENTRING:

The Desert Fathers and Mothers:
Wild silence in a toxic culture

Wherever you go, keep God in mind; whatever you do,
follow the example of Holy Scripture; wherever you are,
stay there and do not move away in a hurry. If you keep to
these guide-lines, you will be saved. (Anthony of the Desert,
AD 251–356)

By the end of the third century AD, Christianity had grown, in spite of brutal persecution, from a provincial Jewish sect into the dominant faith of the Roman Empire. And then, in the year 312, the unthinkable happened and Emperor Constantine himself converted to Christianity (though his sincerity is questionable). Roman temples were quickly converted into churches, pagan feast days became Christian festivals, and a faith once despised and reviled became socially advantageous. Christians acquired status and the Church acquired power.

But many Christians were deeply disturbed. Recalling the humility and simplicity of Jesus, they worried that his followers were being corrupted, his gospel diluted and his holy bride exploited. Refusing to conform, they determined to seek out a simpler, humbler, holier way of life, far away from the corrupting centres of power, in the Egyptian and Syrian wilderness.

They became known as the Desert Fathers and Mothers. At the heart of their spirituality was spiritual warfare (Chapter 11) and an approach to prayer known as 'hesychasm' (from the Greek for 'stillness, rest, quiet, silence'). This is the practice of 'interior silence and continual prayer' that we've been exploring in this chapter.

Surprisingly, having fled the world, these men and women now began to change it. Their lives of austerity, militant spirituality and continual prayer spoke prophetically to the jaded culture of their day. Hundreds of pilgrims sought to learn from the wise insights of people like Anthony of the Desert. 'It was as if a physician had been given by God to Egypt', says Athanasius, his biographer. 'For who in grief met Anthony and did not return rejoicing?'[20] Counter-cultural communities and economies began to form around these prayer warriors, and the first monasteries were born. Missionaries began to travel north from the Egyptian deserts, carrying the gospel, planting radical monastic settlements and evangelising the Celtic peoples of Britain at least two centuries before the Roman Church arrived at Canterbury.

Thomas Merton, who himself abandoned a sophisticated life in New York City to become a Trappist monk, says of the Desert pioneers: 'They knew that they were helpless to do any good for others as long as they floundered about in the wreckage. But once they got a foothold on solid ground, things were different. Then they had not only the power but even the obligation to pull the whole world to safety after them.'[21]

> Sit in thy cell and thy cell will teach thee all.
> (Abba Moses)

STEP 2: REJOICE
Adoration & Thanksgiving

Rejoice in the Lord always.
I will say it again: rejoice! (Phil. 4:4)

No one stares up at the Northern Lights thinking, 'Wow, I'm incredible!' We are hardwired to wonder and therefore to worship. The Lord's Prayer begins with an invitation to adoration: 'Our Father in heaven, hallowed be your name.' Having paused to be still at the start of a prayer time, the most natural and appropriate response to God's presence is reverence. Try not to skip this bit. Hallowing the Father's name is the most important and enjoyable dimension of prayer. Linger here, rejoicing in God's blessings before asking for any more. Like an eagle soaring, a horse galloping or a salmon leaping, worship is the thing God's designed you to do.

4: Adoration

How to worship God

'Our Father in heaven,
hallowed be your name.'

———————————

Prayer is more than you can ever imagine, because
God is so much beyond what you can conceive.
We are surrounded with gods that are too small to
be up to the task of holding our deepest longings,
never mind the world's most urgent problems.
(David G. Benner)[1]

In a quiet Umbrian town many years ago a wealthy lawyer heard reports of a twenty-five-year-old ex-soldier called Giovanni, who had recently given everything he owned to the poor. Was he mad, or had he really experienced some kind of epiphany? Everyone in the town had their own opinion.

Determining to find out for himself, Bernard of Quintavalle invited Giovanni to stay the night and stationed himself to spy on his guest through a secret peep-hole. As the house fell silent he watched in amazement as Giovanni sprang from his bed, knelt down and began to repeat a single, simple phrase again and again: 'My God and my all. My God and my all.' Tears ran down his cheeks. 'My God and my all.'

Bernard of Quintavalle was so inspired by Giovanni's self-evident, all-consuming love for the Lord that he followed his example, gave away his wealth and became the young man's first disciple. Within a year there were eleven of them. Within a decade there were more than five thousand. And within

twenty years the course of European history had been realigned
by the joyous life and simple teaching of Francis of Assisi, as
Giovanni is better known today. The political activist Jim Wallis
says that 'Francis of Assisi returned to the gospel with such
force that it shook the whole world.'[2] The Marxist leader Lenin
said, 'Give me ten men like Francis of Assisi and I will rule the
world', which is ironic because Francis and his followers never
wanted to rule the world, having relinquished money, power
and worldly prestige. Theirs was a revolution founded not on
domination but on adoration: the compelling simplicity of a
fully surrendered life that cries out night and day, 'My God and
my all.'

Our Father

*All who adore him must adore him in the Spirit of Truth. And day
and night let us direct praises and prayers to him, saying, 'Our Father,
who art in heaven.'* (Francis of Assisi)[3]

It's easy to skim through the opening line of the Lord's Prayer
as if it's just some kind of pleasantry – a heavenly handshake,
a ding-dong at the door, before we get down to the real business
of asking – but nothing could be further from the truth.

MOST PEOPLE'S BIGGEST PROBLEM WITH PRAYER IS GOD

The way we view God affects everything about everything, and
the primary purpose of our lives, according to the very first
statement of the Westminster Shorter Catechism, 'is to glorify
God and enjoy him forever'. Every other line of the Lord's Prayer
is both pre-empted and primed by its eight opening words of
adoration: 'Our Father in heaven, hallowed be your name.'

When Jesus told his disciples to address God in this way
they would have been surprised to say the least. They knew
that their Scriptures occasionally compared Yahweh to a father,
but would never before have dared to address him directly in

such familiar – and familial – terms. Jesus was inviting his disciples to step into a level of intimacy with God that they had never before imagined possible.

After more than twenty-five years in pastoral ministry, twenty of them teaching on prayer, I have come to the conclusion that most people's biggest problem with prayer is God. They envisage him scowling, perpetually disapproving, invariably disappointed and needing to be placated or persuaded in prayer. If that's how you picture God, I really don't blame you for trying to avoid his gaze! But Jesus says something completely different. He makes it clear, in his parable of the Prodigal, that the God to whom we pray is extravagantly kind; a father who comes running towards us with arms flung wide, *whenever* we approach him, *wherever* we've been and *whatever* we've done. He assures us that Yahweh, the Holy One of Israel, the Creator of the cosmos, the sustainer of the universe is (drumroll please) *on our side*.

The deeper we receive our identity as 'dearly loved children',[4] the greater our desire to spend time with our Father in prayer. We will start to tell him everything and dare to ask him anything because we now know that, as Jesus puts it elsewhere, 'Your Father in heaven [loves to] give good gifts to those who ask him.'[5] Isn't that amazing? God *wants* to bless you. He is lovingly attentive to your needs, always pleased to see you, predisposed to answer the cries of your heart.[6]

* * *

As a little boy, Danny would often grip big, wax crayons in his chubby little fist to draw 'words' on any scrap of paper he could find. 'Daddy,' he said one day, handing me his latest masterpiece, 'look what I writed.'

'Wow!' I said, as if he'd knocked off the first page of *Macbeth*. 'Well done, Danny. That's so *clever*! You're writing so *beautifully*.'

'Wrong way up, silly,' he replied.

'Oh, right.' I spun the paper and studied it again. 'Daniel,' I said eventually, 'you have written a great, big, long *letter* here, haven't you?' He looked extremely pleased. So pleased that he uttered two words that stopped my heart: 'Read it!'

I stared at that crumpled piece of paper searching for a clue. Should I break it to him that his scribbles, while beautiful in their own way, didn't actually say anything? Would he feel deceived? Discouraged? Could I distract him? Should I change the subject? 'Read it Daddy,' the little voice commanded again.

Looking up from the paper I stared in wild despair at the little face in front of me and suddenly knew exactly what to do. His scribbles remained incomprehensible, but his face was an open book. I knew its every wrinkle, contour and nuance, its every fleeting mood. It told me more eloquently than poetry and prose the kind of day he'd had, how he was feeling, what he'd eaten for dinner, and which weird little obsessions were currently buzzing around his head like bluebottles in a jar.

I returned to my son's artistry, cleared my throat, and began to read aloud. He listened intently, clearly surprised by his own brilliance and chuckling heartily in all the right places. 'Well done, Daddy,' he said in the end, emphasising each word with an emphatic nod of his head. 'That was' – he nodded twice – 'Very. Good. Reading.' And he nodded three more times.

'Well, thank you,' I said, nodding my head too, because it really had been some of the very best reading I had ever done.

Our Father in heaven doesn't get distracted by our scribbled words and squiggled thoughts. He isn't impressed by the dictionaries and lectionaries we hurl at the sky. Instead, he explores our hearts with infinite affection to discern the kind of day we've had, the way we are really feeling and the weird little obsessions buzzing around our heads like bluebottles in a jar. 'God's ear hears the heart's voice,' said Augustine in his commentary on Psalm 148.[7] 'It is the heart that prays', said Father Jean-Nicolas Grou in the eighteenth century. 'It is to the voice of the heart that God listens, and it is the heart that he answers.'[8] 'We do not know what we ought to pray for,' admits the Apostle Paul, 'but the Spirit himself intercedes for us through wordless groans. And he who searches our hearts knows the mind of the Spirit.'[9]

Isn't it a relief to learn that the Father 'searches our hearts' the way I searched Danny's face that day? You may well question the coherence of those scribbles and squiggles you present to him as prayer, you may doubt the strength of your own resolve and the sincerity of your faith, but at least try to trust that the Spirit's translation of your prayers stands a pretty good chance of getting through to the Father's heart on your behalf!

> Lord, help me not to worry about the words, but address you with the language of the heart . . . I simply present myself to you; I open my heart to you . . . Teach me to pray. Amen.
> (François Fénelon, 1651–1715)

Hallowed be your name

There's an exquisite symmetry in the way that Jesus counterpoints the emphasis of his first four words, 'Our Father in heaven', with that of the next four, 'hallowed be your name'. As the biblical scholar William Barclay says, this 'saves the idea of the Fatherhood of God from all sentimentality and . . . sets down in unmistakable terms the inescapable obligation of reverence'.[10]

I said earlier that after twenty-five years in pastoral ministry I have come to the conclusion that many people struggle with prayer simply because they doubt that God likes them. But there are probably just as many of us who fail to fully grasp his holiness. We have a notion of divine love devoid of divine sovereignty. Unwittingly we have unhallowed the Father's name. And in losing the Godness of God we struggle with prayer because we fail to grasp the mind-blowing privilege of simply being in the presence of the living God. Familiarity breeds apathy until we can barely be bothered to try.

Pulitzer Prize-winning author Annie Dillard describes the lunacy of such over-familiarity:

Does anyone have the foggiest idea what sort of power we so
blithely invoke? Or, as I suspect, does no one believe a word
of it? . . . It is madness to wear ladies' straw hats and velvet
hats to church; we should all be wearing crash helmets. Ushers
should issue life preservers and signal flares; they should lash
us to our pews.[11]

The first Christians may not have donned crash helmets in
worship, but they certainly understood the sovereignty of God
in a way that we don't or can't or won't. Scan the narrative of
Acts, reflect upon the spontaneous doxologies of Paul, or the
apocalypse of John, and you quickly come to the conclusion
that their God was – frankly – bigger than ours. They knew
how to kneel. They understood the 'fear of the Lord', the reverence he deserves, and even the 'dreadful thing' it can sometimes
be, as the writer of Hebrews says, 'to fall into the hands of the
living God'.[12]

Insha'Allah

I have always liked the way that Muslims and many Middle-
Eastern Christians add *Insha'Allah* – 'if God wills' – to their
plans. In so doing they acknowledge that God's will and wisdom
are at work in all things and at all times, subsuming ours. In
many parts of the West we have lost this sense of *Insha'Allah.*
We have God all wrapped up in Bible verses – hooked up on
a tight scriptural leash. There is no mystery, only certainty in
our religion.

I meet well-meaning people like this everywhere I go. When
they hear that my wife is sick they urge me, with extraordinary
levels of eye-contact, to pray for her in some better way, or to
break off some random curse, or to have her repent of a
particular attitude, or to take a particular nutritional supplement,
or to visit a particular healing ministry, or to stand on our heads
with a garlic clove in each ear singing the 'Hallelujah Chorus'.
Compared to these people I sometimes feel feeble with all my
questions, my frayed faith, my stumbling down the corridor at

night, fumbling for the bathroom light. Sometimes I envy them. I eye the garlic and search for Handel's *Messiah*.

But I can't help feeling that their God (or is it their god?) is just a bit too . . . neat – a plastic dashboard Jesus, bobbing his head along to whatever music we choose to play. C.S. Lewis, whose divine archetype, Aslan, was famously 'not a tame lion', once said, 'The longer I am a Christian, and the closer I draw to God, the less discernible is His will.'[13]

I'M STUCK WITH GOD, EVEN WHEN I DON'T UNDERSTAND HIM. EVEN WHEN I DON'T COMPLETELY LIKE HIM. TURNS OUT HE IS ALL I'VE GOT

I don't understand why Sammy has not yet been fully healed (God knows, we have prayed). I definitely don't understand why he does some miracles and not others – it often seems so arbitrary. But I am learning to understand that I may never fully understand. I am learning to be a bit more OK with not being OK. Life sometimes hurts like hell but I've discovered that deleting God from the equation doesn't actually help. It merely removes all meaning and morality from the mess, and all real hope from the future. And so I'm sort of stuck with God, even when I don't understand him. Even when I don't completely like him. Turns out he is all I've got. And maybe this is where hallowing actually begins.

Living with a wild God
The social scientist Barbara Ehrenreich wrote a bewildering, and beautiful book about her journey of spiritual awakening and called it *Living with a Wild God*. It's a good book but the best thing about it is definitely the title. What's the point of a divinity you can fit on a thumb-drive, a bumper sticker or within a human skull? The God of the cosmos must surely be bigger than our capacity to understand?

My father died when I was relatively young and perhaps that's

why I have always found great comfort in the idea of God as
my heavenly Father, an ever-present Dad on call. The Spirit within
sparks this beautiful cry 'Abba' as deep unto deep. We are prod-
igals loved. And yet I am also increasingly finding comfort, and
an unexpected intimacy, in God's hiddenness. His otherness. The
very fact that our Father is in heaven and not here on earth.

I walk outside at night and feel insignificant yet connected;
part of something transcendent and vast. I whisper my prayers
beneath the silent star-fields, sensing that I am reaching the
divinity within all this mystery in a way that my loudest, most
desperate and defiant shouts might not. God seems infinitely
close, dangerous yet familiar, faithful but unpredictable, loving
but not necessarily nice.

After being told again and again over the years how deeply
God loves me, 'as if no one else existed', and how powerfully
he wants to use me – 'Hey, we can all be history makers!' – it
comes as a considerable relief to finally discover that I'm actually not that big a deal. A bit-part actor – certainly not the lead
– in the play of someone else's life. I am, as the Psalmist says,
just dust. I am, as Isaiah says, like grass that grows, withers
and dies in a day. I am a child who finally knows enough to
know that I don't know much, and that it's perfectly possible
to trust in things I don't fully understand. Perhaps it's better
after all to have a mustard seed than a mountain. I'd rather
have a little faith in a great, big unshakable God than a great,
big unshakable faith in a little god unworthy of the title.

You may very well be thinking by now, 'It's all very well to tell
stories about your kid learning to write and Francis of Assisi,
but I'm not exactly a saint. I find worship difficult at the best
of times.' So let's look at a few simple, practical ways to worship
God even when you don't feel like it.

1. Awaking my soul
If adoration fails to erupt spontaneously when I first approach
God in prayer, I take hold of my soul quite firmly and make it

wake up! I love the way George MacDonald puts it in his *The Diary of an Old Soul*, 'We who would be born again indeed must wake our souls unnumbered times a day and urge ourselves to life with holy greed.'[14] This is precisely what King David does in Psalm 103: 'Praise the LORD, my soul,' he says, commanding his own sluggish soul to wake up and worship. 'All my inmost being, praise his holy name.'

This is an act of the will. Instead of waiting to worship until I feel like it (which could be a very long wait indeed), I begin to thank God for all the evidence of his love in my life – often speaking out loud – until my feelings fall into line with the facts. Sometimes this can seem a bit fake at first, but that's OK. And occasionally I continue to feel tired, sad or lethargic, and that's OK too. If I only said 'I love you' to my wife when I was overwhelmed with passion, I wouldn't tell her often enough! And actually my love for her may well be more honest – less fake – in the cold light of an ordinary day than it is during the hormonal surge of an emotional moment. The writer of Hebrews urges us to 'offer to God a sacrifice of praise'.[15] What could be more sacrificial than praising him when we don't feel like it? It's relatively easy to worship when we're singing stirring songs with the saints on Sunday morning, but not so easy on a miserable Monday morning before work. I suspect that unemotional worship – the kind that feels a bit forced and fake – is precious to God precisely because it is so costly to us.

2. Praying a Psalm

One of the easiest ways of building adoration into my own prayer life is simply to read a Psalm (or part of a longer one) every morning and every evening. It never ceases to amaze me that this is the very same prayer book that Jesus used and loved, and that much of it is three thousand years old, written by King David himself. Why would I not use such a priceless resource daily? I often find that my feelings and priorities are realigned as the Psalms draw me into a worldview older and stranger than my own.

It's fascinating that so many of these prayers seem to have been written for use at particular times of the day. For example, Psalm 4 is clearly the prayer of a person preparing themselves for bed: 'In peace I will lie down and sleep, for you alone, Lord, make me dwell in safety' (v. 8). But its successor, Psalm 5, is a prayer for the start of a new day: 'In the morning, Lord, you hear my voice; in the morning I lay my requests before you and wait expectantly' (v. 3). The very first Psalm describes the blessing of meditating 'day and night' on God's word (1:2).

I find it helpful to read Psalms aloud whenever possible, because this is how they would first have been used and it helps to stir my soul. As I do so, I look out for a particular phrase or line that resonates with my heart and, once I find one, I try to memorise it and revisit it in idle moments during the day. (You can find out more about how to *Pray the Psalms* in the Tool-shed section online.)

3. Worshipping with Bach, Beyoncé and Bethel

As well as praying the Psalms, I try to fill my day with music. Melody and harmony are God-given gifts that can stir the human soul more powerfully than any other external stimulus. I'm slightly embarrassed to admit that, in 24–7 prayer rooms, I'm partial to either techno (great for intercession), or the harmonies of Giovanni Pierluigi da Palestrina, whose music may well have been inspired by the polyphonic sounds of monks singing in tongues. When I'm hill-walking, I find myself turning to the grandeur of great, old hymns. One of the finest jazz records of all time – *A Love Supreme* by John Coltrane – is a journey into the mystery of God. Many of the greatest classical compositions in the world are deeply worshipful. I am listening as I type to the celestial sounds of *Spem in Alium* by Thomas Tallis. When it comes to worship, instrumental music has the added advantage of bypassing the left hemisphere of the brain's central cortex, enabling our spirits to soar unencumbered by the constraints of language.

4. Worshipping with others

You've probably noticed that the entire Lord's Prayer is written in the plural. Its very first word is addressed to 'Our' Father in heaven. Not my father. Not your father. Ours. This is a family thing. 'Give *us our* daily bread . . . forgive *us our* sins' and so on. When we pray the Lord's Prayer we do so corporately, in community with others – not just personally and spontaneously but liturgically in unison with millions of Christians around the world today, and in fellowship with the communion of saints stretching back to those first twelve apostles gathered around Christ as he gave them this prayer. We are not designed to hallow the Father's name entirely on our own. It's not enough just to download resources for solitary prayer and worship from the internet. We all need the encouragement, the challenge and the discomfort of active participation in a local worshipping community.

5. Liturgy: the shape and the shaping of our prayers

There was a season of my life when I just couldn't face attending the kind of free-styling charismatic worship service my own church was serving up at that time. Sammy was incredibly unwell, and my heart was simply too vulnerable to run the gauntlet of spontaneity every week. And so I found myself rising early on Sundays to sneak away to our local Anglican cathedral for a short, anonymous service of Holy Communion in that great, fan-vaulted, ancient barn. I hoped no one would recognise me. I was meant to be leading one of the wildest, most charismatic, least traditional congregations in town. After the services I would sometimes pull a hoody over my head as if I were leaving a strip club rather than a cathedral. I was embarrassed to find myself sampling and even appreciating the kind of liturgy we had often denounced as 'dead religion', or 'vain repetition'.

And yet I kept returning for several months because I valued the way that every word of every service in this ancient building seemed to matter. Nothing was left to chance. When your soul is spent and you've run out of imagination and initiative it's a relief to be told what to say by someone you trust. I also appreciated the sense of being part of something very old – bigger than my own chaotic predicament and stronger than my own brittle resolve. It was a relief to be sedated by the predictability of the lectionary, the serene circadian cycles of ecclesiastical routine.

It was an important season but, as my heart recovered, I began to miss the familiar joy of free-flowing worship, and of church built on relationships, and of ministry in the power of the Holy Spirit. These days I continue to value set prayers and services alongside spontaneous approaches. My own prayer life blends speaking in tongues and chatting to God informally through the day, with the Ignatian prayer of *Examen* (see Chapter 10), regular monastic retreats, the sixteenth-century Book of Common Prayer, and even membership of a religious Order.[16] I am convinced that liturgy as an expression of worship belongs just as much to the two-thousand-year-old charismatic free church tradition as it does to anyone else.

I WOULD PULL A HOODY OVER MY HEAD AS IF I WERE LEAVING A STRIP CLUB RATHER THAN A CATHEDRAL

Authentic worship is anchored in biblical realities greater than our own mercurial temperaments. We see this in the life of Jesus, who paused conscientiously three times a day to recite the *sh'ma* ('Hear O Israel . . .') and to give thanks before meals.[17] His own book of fixed worship – the Psalms – was so deeply ingrained in his psyche that he even quoted it from the cross.

Thoughtful prayers written by others, and especially those written in the Bible, can enable us to express things we find difficult and to address things we might otherwise ignore. If I only ever 'chat to God about the things on my heart' I will very rarely remember, for instance, to obey Paul's command to uphold our political leaders in prayer.[18] In the first chapter I said that one of the great things about having a fixed place for prayer is that it gives you somewhere to show up even when you don't want to pray! Liturgy can be the verbal equivalent of such a location. It gives your prayers a certain architecture – a consistent framework – even when you don't want to pray, or don't know how to pray, or can't find the words to express your heart. By choosing to use a fixed prayer you say to God, 'I don't know what else to say, right now, and I don't really feel like worshipping, but here is my offering anyway.'

'There's much to be said for Christianity as repetition', says the theologian Stanley Hauerwas. 'Evangelicalism doesn't have enough repetition in a way that will form Christians to survive in a world that constantly tempts us to always think we have to do something new.'[19] When we repeat fixed prayers, several thousand years of faith begin to shape us and pray through us, providing solidarity (in every sense of that word) amid the subjectivity of our fragmenting culture, with all God's people. Going through the motions, as every dancer knows, can be an important thing to do.

Our friend Sabina trained hard most days of her childhood and into adult life with a dream of becoming a ballerina. After years of hard work she finally achieved her ambition, making it onto the world stage as a dancer for the Royal Ballet before retiring in her late twenties. But now that Sabina has swapped her ballet shoes for the Ugg boots of motherhood, it's fascinating to watch the enduring elegance with which she moves. It doesn't matter what she's doing – washing the dishes or changing a nappy – she carries herself like poetry. Dance is no longer something she does, but it is still something she is.

I have another friend who was mentored by an extraordinarily godly, eloquent man who eventually, in old age, slipped into dementia. He grew increasingly muddled and would lose his thread in conversation. But whenever he prayed it was almost as if he'd been healed! All the old fluency, wisdom and fire returned. Suddenly he was sharp as a pin. Somehow the prayers he had spoken, again and again over so many years, seemed at last to be speaking him.

Like a dancer becoming the dance, and a pastor becoming the prayer, we are all being transformed into the likeness of Christ . . . 'with ever-increasing glory'.[20] Like a butterfly emerging from a chrysalis, our metamorphosis comes through the constraints of holy habits, the training of neural pathways, the set prayers and the spiritual practices we maintain in our lives.

6. Worshipping with your own weirdness

Where and when did you last feel close to God? Try to identify and pursue the particular people and places, the music and activities. that speak the mother-tongue of your heart. By prioritising these things, you will live with greater joy. For the Olympian athlete Eric Liddell it was running. 'God made me fast,' he said, 'and when I run, I feel his pleasure!' King David was moved to worship by the night sky: 'When I consider your heavens, the work of your fingers, the moon and the stars, which you have set in place . . .' (Ps. 8:3). The craftsman Bezalel, who was commissioned to decorate the tabernacle, glorified God with his artistic skills.[21] Mary uttered her Magnificat, one of the greatest worship prayers of all time, in response to the wonder of her own pregnancy. The magi were led to Jesus by intellectual pursuit.

My soul is awakened by climbing mountains, by particular writers, and by certain friends whose company consistently points me back to Jesus. Time spent enjoying such pleasures is something my soul requires. I don't do these things just because they are nice but because they are necessary. It is a matter of rigorous spiritual discipline, therefore, to make space in my life for the great outdoors, for T.S. Eliot, Annie Dillard and R.S. Thomas, for big sloshing mugs of tea with friends like Phil, Jill and Mike, Scot, Ken and Tim. These people help me to hallow the Father's name in deep humanity.

Of course, you will be wired to worship differently. Having encouraged you (in Chapter 2) to discover your own distinctive ways of praying, I am now urging you to do the same with adoration. The Psalmist exhorts us on five separate occasions to 'sing to the Lord a new song' because he wants us to worship spontaneously, creatively and from the heart. You are a new song that God has given to the world; a song that no one else can sing. The way you think, the way you see life, and the way you worship is utterly unique! Isn't it time you stepped out of the karaoke bar, out onto the street, threw back your head and gave the world the weirdest, most wonderful rendition of you?

In this chapter we have seen that the way we approach God in prayer, and the way we view him in life, affects everything about everything. He is a loving Father who greets us with a smile and not a scowl, who sees our hearts and interprets our scribbled prayers. But he is also 'in heaven' and 'hallowed' – sovereign, awesome and mysterious, which means that we can trust him even when we don't understand him. The invitation to adoration means greeting our heavenly Father by name, meeting his smile with a smile, receiving him as the loved one he truly is, responding to his kindness with kindness, his presence with presence, and his love with our own. In a world that forsakes and despises him continually, what joy we can bring to the Father's heart! As we move now from 'Rejoicing' to the third step of our prayer process, 'Asking', we do so with a deep awareness that God is good and that we are loved.

MORE ON ADORATION:

- **PRAYER COURSE SESSION**: #2: Adoration.

- **PRAYER TOOLS**: 1. How to Pray the Psalms. 2. How to Practise Christian Meditation. 3. How to Pray Creatively. 4. How to Practise the Presence of God (prayercourse.org).

- **FURTHER READING**: *The Practice of the Presence of God*, by Brother Lawrence.

HERO OF ADORATION:

Brother Lawrence: *Practising the presence*

There is not in the world a way of life more sweet, nor more delightful than continual conversation with God.[22]

A middle-aged injured soldier called Nicolas Herman was staring at a tree in winter, its leaves stripped bare, reflecting that it was how he felt too. Remembering that – though the tree looked dead – it would burst into new life in the spring, he experienced an overwhelming sense of hope. Nicolas joined a Carmelite monastery in Paris in 1651, changed his name to Brother Lawrence, and spent the rest of his life there doing menial jobs in the kitchen, and latterly mending sandals. The self-described 'big clumsy fellow who broke everything' learned lessons about living a life of worship and 'practicing the presence of God' in the ordinary, which have enriched countless Christians ever since.

'As often as I could,' he says, 'I placed myself as a worshipper before him, fixing my mind upon his holy presence, recalling it when I found it wandering from him. This proved to be an exercise frequently painful, yet I persisted through all difficulties.'

For almost five hundred years, Brother Lawrence has been inspiring people to stay focused on God's presence in their everyday lives. 'Is it not quicker and easier', he asks, 'just to do our common business wholly for the love of him? . . . (For) even the smallest remembrance will always please him.'

'It is not necessary for being with God to be always at church; we may make an oratory of our heart wherein to retire from time to time, to converse with him . . . Everyone is capable of such familiar conversation with God.'

STEP 3: ASK

Petition, Intercession & Perseverance

Your kingdom come, your will be done on earth as in heaven. Give us today our daily bread.

Prayer means many things to many people, but at its simplest and most immediate it means asking God for help. It's a soldier begging for courage, a football fan at the final, a mother alone in a hospital chapel. The Lord's Prayer invites us to ask God for everything from 'daily bread' to the 'kingdom come', for ourselves ('petition') and for others ('intercession'). In this section, we explore the extraordinary, miracle-working power of prayer, but also the questions we face when our prayers go unanswered.

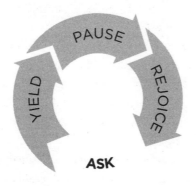

5: Petition

How to ask God

'Give us today our daily bread.'

The Lord's Prayer begins and ends with adoration, but in the middle it's a shopping list of requests for God's kingdom to come, the provision of daily bread, forgiveness of sins and deliverance from evil. In this part of the book we are going to focus on three particular aspects of asking. First, in this chapter, we're going to look at petition, which is primarily asking God to meet our own needs. In the next chapter we'll consider intercession, which is asking God on behalf of other people. And then, in the final chapter of this section, we're going to focus on the difficult issue of unanswered prayer. Although almost every line of the Lord's Prayer is asking for something, I have chosen to lift 'Give us today our daily bread' out of its natural sequence and to use it here, because it so perfectly illustrates petition. We will return to the natural order of the prayer in the following chapters as we turn our attention to intercession 'your kingdom come' and unanswered prayer 'your will be done'.

* * *

Some of our closest friends invited us to join them in Croatia, sailing a catamaran around the Adriatic. It was to be the holiday of a lifetime. By day we ploughed through sapphire seas under powder-blue skies, weaving in and out of the dramatic Kornati archipelago. At night we moored in perfect coves, diving, swimming and playing cards by lamplight under the brightest stars you ever saw. It was a magical week.

One evening we dropped anchor in a particularly beautiful natural harbour, and the kids dived into the sea as usual. By the time we'd hauled them out, wrapped them in soft towels and settled down to supper, dusk was bathing the entire bay in a golden sheen. Everyone looked relaxed, tanned and happy. Everything was perfect until a dark, swirling cloud of mosquitoes materialised above our heads.

I'm aware, as I recount this story, that you may not be entirely sympathetic to our plight. You may even be thinking 'Good!' and praising God for those mosquitoes, but back on that boat we most definitely were not. In fact, my friend James immediately began to pray against them. 'Lord,' he said, lifting one hand like Moses preparing to part the Red Sea, and using the other to swat his own face, 'We ask you to just remove these wretched mozzies, right now, in the name of Jesus.'

Everyone else on the boat – two mums, five kids – heartily agreed with this prayer. Their eyes were closed, heads nodding, hands raised to rebuke Satan's little air-born militia. But my eyes were not closed, my head did not nod, because it seemed such a silly prayer for three important reasons.

My first objection was *theological*. God must surely be a bit too busy with Big World Problems (like the Middle East and wars and famines and stuff) to worry about optimising the *al fresco* dining arrangements of posh people on yachts in the Adriatic.

My second objection was *environmental*. Mosquitoes are presumably part of God's finely tuned ecological order and Christians aren't immune from the laws of nature. We don't surrender our insect-repellents at conversion. We don't rise from the baptismal waters and keep rising, liberated from the laws of gravity.

My third objection was *pastoral*. Our kids were joining in with James's prayer, and so when (not if) it didn't work, tiny grains of doubt and disappointment would surely be sown within their impressionable minds and they would grow up to become Satanists.

And so, as everyone else prayed, rebuking the spirit of

midgey-ness in the name of Jesus, I smiled stoically, swatting mosquitoes until they all said, 'Amen'. But as they did so, the most annoying and unfortunate thing occurred. At that precise moment a gentle breeze arose and swept the mosquitoes away to some other, doubtless less prayerful, yacht. A chorus of praise erupted from our boat. Everyone was suddenly grinning and thanking God for hearing their prayers, for caring about his kids and, yes, for making the night's perfect *al fresco* dining arrangements just that little bit more perfect.

WHEN YOU PRAY ABOUT THE SMALL THINGS IN LIFE, YOU GET TO LIVE WITH GREATER GRATITUDE

To this day, I don't know whether that was an actual, proper answer to prayer or just a well-timed meteorological fluke masquerading as one, but this I do know, and I know it for sure: when you pray about the small things in life, you get to live with greater gratitude. If you only ever pray about big, ugly, gnarly problems that seem onerous and serious enough to warrant divine intervention, you will only very occasionally experience miracles. But when you learn to pray about trivia – ridiculous incidentals like 'Lead us not into temptation but deliver us from evil midges', and even inevitabilities like 'Give us this day our daily bread' (in a land that's full of the stuff) – you start to notice how many minor miracles are scattered abroad in the course of an average day. As Archbishop William Temple famously said, 'When I pray, coincidences happen; when I stop praying, the coincidences stop happening.'[1] It is by asking more for lesser things that we rediscover how to live with the wide-eyed wonder of children. By filling our days with tiny prayers, we relinquish our sense of entitlement and receive each detail as a blessing, each coincidence as a minor miracle, training our neural pathways to 'rejoice always, pray continually, give thanks in all circumstances; for this is God's will for you in Christ Jesus'.[2]

Praying for parking spaces

One of the greatest theological questions of our time in the realm
of petitionary prayer appears to be whether or not we should
ask God for parking spaces. I've seen rooms light up with debate
on this one thorny conundrum. And it seems to me that the
answer is clear: yes, we should indeed ask God to give us parking
spots. Why? Because when we pray for places to park we become
the kind of people who worship God for a patch of concrete
outside a supermarket on a rainy Saturday in January.

'OK,' you say, 'but would you have got that parking space if
you hadn't asked God for it? Did it only become available when
you prayed?' And my answer to your excellent question is that
I honestly don't know, and I honestly don't care. I'm sure there
are clever theologians, philosophers and quantum physicists
out there who can enlighten us but, in the meantime, while
they tweak their calculations and analyse the original Greek
manuscripts, I am trying to be less cynical, more prayerful, like
my friend James rebuking the mosquitoes. James certainly
knows how to pray big prayers about grave human suffering
because he works at the forefront of the fight against human
trafficking. But he also prays tiny prayers about trivial things
with a beautiful, childlike faith.

The law of asking

Prayer means many things to many people, but at its simplest
and most obvious it means asking God for help. This is how
most non-churchgoers and all children understand the word,
and they're right. The word 'pray' comes from the Middle
English 'to ask earnestly' and the Latin *precari*, which means
'to entreat'. Absolutely everyone prays in this way from time
to time. There are no atheists on a falling plane. It really is the
most natural thing in the world to ask God for a safe landing,
or for healing, guidance, forgiveness, provision, protection, or
a parking space at the supermarket on a wet November day.

The Lord's Prayer is punctuated with precisely this kind of
personal, practical request: 'Give us . . . Forgive us . . . Lead us

. . . Deliver us.' Elsewhere Jesus says, 'Ask me for anything in my name and I will do it',[3] and, on another occasion, 'Ask and it will be given to you; seek and you will find; knock and the door will be opened to you.'[4] The Apostle James is equally explicit: 'You do not have because you do not ask God.'[5] The Cambridge professor H.H. Farmer says that 'if prayer is the heart of religion, then petition is the heart of prayer',[6] and Karl Barth, one of the greatest theologians of modern times, emphatically agrees:

> It is the fact that [a man] comes before God with his petition which makes him a praying man. Other theories of prayer may be richly and profoundly thought out and may sound very well, but they all suffer from a certain artificiality because they miss this simple and concrete fact, losing themselves in heights and depths where there is no place for the man who really prays, who is simply making a request.[7]

It's fascinating to note that the first half of the Lord's Prayer was not entirely original to Jesus. He seems to have adopted and adapted the opening lines from another contemporary prayer known as the *Kaddish* (one of the three most important prayers in Jewish liturgy)[8], which went like this:

> Magnified and hallowed be his great name,
> In the world which he created according to his will
> And may he establish his kingdom during your life.

The similarities to the Lord's Prayer are striking:

	Our Father, in heaven,
Magnified and hallowed be	Hallowed be
his great name.	your name,
In the world which he created	Your kingdom come,
according to his will	your will be done
and may he establish	on earth as it is
his kingdom during your life.	in heaven.

We shouldn't be surprised that Jesus incorporated traditional
liturgy into his teaching, but it's particularly interesting to note
the lines that he adds, because in them we hear – with a sort
of shock of recognition – Christ's distinctive voice ringing out
above the formal religion of his time.

Where the *Kaddish* is concerned with the vertical axis of
God's greatness and his impending kingdom, Jesus softens this
('Our Father'), and adds his own horizontal axis: a list of simple
petitions for food, safety, protection and forgiveness. He
surrounds the reverence and longing of the original prayer with
relational language and practical requests regarding the everyday
concerns of ordinary people.

Miracles

*Miracle is just a word we use for the things The Powers have deluded
us into thinking that God is unable to do.* (Walter Wink)[9]

Many best-selling experts on prayer disregard the subject of
petition almost entirely. They talk a great deal about the psychological aspects of communion with God – contemplation,
meditation, stillness and silence – but say very little about
simply asking God for help and expecting him to answer.

**OUR PRIMARY PRIVILEGE AS GOD'S CHILDREN
IS TO ASK AUDACIOUSLY AND REPEATEDLY
FOR EVERYTHING WE NEED, EXPECTING HIM
TO ANSWER, NATURALLY OR SUPERNATURALLY**

They lose themselves, as Barth says, 'in heights and depths
where there is no place for the man who . . . is simply making
a request'. An ageing monk once admitted to me that he doesn't
pray about his own personal, practical needs. He asks God to
help him become an answer to his own prayers but doesn't
expect or request any other kind of miracle. I was too polite to
suggest that this might be unchristian.

There is a great deal to be learned and enjoyed in contemplative prayer, as we shall see in Chapter 8, and it is certainly true that we can become the answer to our own prayers, but the Bible also insists upon miracles. From the first day of creation to the last chapter of Revelation, Scripture describes God breaking in, invading space and time, interrupting and disrupting the laws of nature. When sick people came to Jesus, they received more than counselling and a glow of inner peace. They were actually, objectively, physically healed!

Jesus was crucified in the body and resurrected as a walking, talking, huggable man who looked like a gardener and cooked fish on a fire on a beach. Every time we take communion, we celebrate the supernatural intervention of God among the atoms, the systems, the actual physical stuff of our material world. We cannot with any integrity jettison or domesticate our belief in the power of petitionary prayer and still lay claim to any form of Christian orthodoxy. Other aspects of prayer are wonderful, and we shall explore them elsewhere in this book, but our primary privilege as God's children is to ask audaciously and repeatedly for everything we need, expecting him to answer, naturally or supernaturally, by whatever means he sees fit.

Daily bread means daily bread
Few people in modern times have demonstrated the power of petitionary prayer more powerfully and consistently than the nineteenth-century philanthropist and pastor George Müller, who started 117 schools, cared for 10,024 orphans, educated 120,000 children and was accused of 'raising the poor above their natural state'.

His legacy is made even more remarkable by the well-documented fact that, instead of appealing for money and making his financial needs publicly known, Müller trusted God to fund this vast operation purely through the power of prayer, raising more than £90 million in today's money in this way.

With so many mouths to feed, and no conventional fund-raising strategy, George Müller was often forced to take the prayer for daily bread very literally indeed. On one occasion, he stood before 300 hungry orphans gathered for breakfast, knowing that there was no food in the kitchen, and said grace, thanking God in faith for the food 'you are going to give us to eat'.

Suddenly, there was a banging at the door and the local baker entered carrying three huge trays of fresh bread, explaining that he'd been up since two o'clock that morning baking for them. The milkman appeared next, announcing that his cart had broken down outside and wondering if they could use his load of fresh milk? Hundreds of children got their daily bread that morning, washed down with creamy milk. It was a breakfast they would surely remember for the rest of their lives whenever they prayed the Lord's Prayer.[10]

The notion of 'daily bread' harks back to the Old Testament when God fed his people in the wilderness with manna that only remained fresh for a day. There is a strong sense in this phrase, therefore, of asking for today's *needs* rather than tomorrow's *wants*. It's not that there's anything wrong with requesting a nicer car, deliverance from mosquitoes, or three urns of fresh milk. It's just that we have no right to expect or insist upon an unending stream of luxuries. Daily bread means daily bread; Nutella cannot be guaranteed. God invites us to ask him for the basics, but has never promised to make us all millionaires!

Why we need to ask

You may remember the story of a blind beggar called Bartimaeus, who cried out to Jesus for help in the city of Jericho. The crowds tried to shut him up but he refused to be silenced. Hearing the commotion, Jesus asked him a surprising question: 'What do you want me to do for you?'

I can imagine Bartimaeus letting out a little gasp of exasperation. Wasn't his need obvious? Hadn't it been obvious to every man, woman and child who ever passed him by? 'Lord,' he said, 'I want to see!' And so Jesus healed him.[11]

People often ask why we need to pray. Doesn't the Lord

already know our needs? Can't he be trusted to do the right thing regardless? Why on earth do we have to ask? The story of Bartimaeus reveals that it's not enough to sit silently in the crowd wishing for a miracle. 'What do you want me to do for you?' Jesus enquires. He asks us to ask, invites us to articulate our specific needs. 'Whether we like it or not,' says the great Baptist preacher Spurgeon,

> asking is the rule of the Kingdom. If you may have everything by asking in His Name, and nothing without asking, I beg you to see how absolutely vital prayer is. God says to his own son: 'Ask of me and I will give you the nations for your inheritance.' If the royal and divine son cannot be exempted from the rule of asking that he may have, you and I cannot expect the rule to relaxed in our favour.[12]

God asks us to ask for at least three reasons. First, because the act of asking is *relational* in a way that mere wishing is not. Jesus is always more interested in friendship than dispensing blessings to faceless souls. When a haemorrhaging woman touched his cloak, he stopped to identify and speak with her. It wasn't enough to answer her prayer anonymously. Immediately after this, he raised a twelve-year-old girl from the dead and, once again, his primary concern was pastoral: 'Give her something to eat.' If Bartimaeus had been healed in the crowd by the mere vapour of Christ's passing he would never have met Jesus, and we would never have come to learn from his beautiful story.

The second reason that asking is necessary is that it is *vulnerable*. To make a request is to admit to some area of personal need. It extends trust towards the person asked. This may be a very minor act of faith – trusting a shopkeeper to supply a pound of potatoes – or it can be very costly – asking a woman to be your wife, or a doctor to cure your disease. In all its forms, asking is an expression of faith, a way of opening our hearts to believe, and our hands to receive from another person.

Third, asking is *intentional*. It involves the activation of our wills. We are not automatons: mindless bots pre-programmed and powerless to resist the Creator's genetic coding. God respects us too much to ride roughshod over our freewills and loves us too much to force us to do his bidding. He comes where he is welcomed, and waits to answer until he is called.

Freewill and God's will

Petitionary prayer is a logical and exciting consequence of human freewill. It means that our fate is not set. Things can change. We are free to ask, activate and advance God's blessing in any given situation by aligning our wills with God's will, praying 'let your will be done'. The great French philosopher Blaise Pascal said that 'God has instituted prayer to impart to his creatures the dignity of causality.'[13] We are God's partners in the great project of creation, and we exercise this extraordinary privilege primarily through prayerful imagination, and secondarily through practical innovation. We tend to expect the King of kings to be a Great Dictator (and might even prefer him to rule in such a manner), but in fact he is a Great Delegator whose divine nature is not to dominate, subjugate and control, but to serve, listen and empower. We are free to do terrible things, as the news cycle reveals, but brilliantly wonderful things too, imagining, inventing and co-creating new realities in prayer.

THERE ARE WONDERFUL THINGS THAT WILL ONLY HAPPEN IF WE ASK FOR THEM

'God does not act the same way whether we pray or not', says Karl Barth. 'Prayer exerts an influence upon God's action, and even upon his existence.'[14] That word influence is important. We can't control God in prayer because he is God and we are not, but he does allow us to influence him. Neither can we over-rule the sovereign choices of other people, however much we might like to force our friend to repent, or stop our sister dating the sleazebag from college. But although we can't *over-ride* the free-will of others, we can *influence* their choices through prayer.

There are wonderful things that will only happen if we ask for them, and unspeakably terrible things that will prevail unless we harness our wills with God's will to resist them in prayer. 'We are not locked into a pre-set, deterministic future', says Richard Foster. 'Ours is an open, not a closed, universe. We are "co-labourers with God" . . . working with God to determine the outcome of events.'[15]

Praying in the name of Jesus

Asking is essential, but not just any kind of asking. Jesus says, 'Ask anything *in my name*, and I will do it.' Some people take this phrase as a magic formula. They tack 'in the name of Jesus' onto everything they ask, expecting it to add a bit of supernatural fire-power to their prayers. But this is not what Jesus meant at all. To pray in the name of Jesus means asking for things that are consistent with his character and aligned with his purpose. When my prayers line up with God's plan for my life, he says 'yes', and when they don't he says 'no'. What a relief! If every earnest, heartfelt prayer I'd ever prayed had been answered, I'd have become a zoo-keeper, and married the wrong girl at least four times before meeting Sammy.

Praying in the name of Jesus means wanting what God wants, aligning our wills with his will, our words with his word, and our personal preferences with his eternal and universal purposes. It also speaks of family privilege. To ask in the name of Jesus is to approach the Father in the company of his own dear Son.

When our boys were still very small I sometimes had to leave them for a couple of weeks at a time for protracted tours of America and Asia-Pacific. On one occasion when Danny, our youngest son, seemed particularly upset about me leaving, I made a big show of writing down my phone number on a post-it note and promising to answer whenever he called. With hindsight, this was a dumb thing to promise, not just because intercontinental calls are expensive but because Danny didn't have any notion of time zones. For two weeks I took calls at night to discuss the adventures of his toys, I dashed out of important meetings to receive detailed updates on his potty training. Danny enjoyed direct access to me at any time of the day or night in a way that no one else does, because he is my son, and because I had promised to take his calls. Our Father in heaven has made the same promise and given us the same direct access through Jesus his Son.[16]

Praying in faith

When Tinker Bell is poisoned by the dastardly Captain Hook in one of the theatrical renditions of *Peter Pan*, the audience is told, 'She's going to die unless we do something. Clap your hands and say "I believe in fairies!"' Some people think that prayer is just faith in faith, positive thinking, clapping for fairies. But people like blind Bartimaeus and George Müller demonstrate that Christian prayer is not wishing but asking, actively addressing specific requests to an actual person. They don't have faith in faith itself, but rather trust in the one who said, 'If you believe, you will receive whatever you ask for in prayer.'[17]

The doctrine of faith has been terribly abused by certain wings of the Church where greed has been glorified and the poor have been oppressed by a heresy known as 'the prosperity gospel'. Preachers promising health and wealth reduce prayer to a form of positive thinking and God himself to a sort of celestial algorithm.

Great damage is done by such unbalanced teaching on faith, but we must not over-react. Jesus tells Bartimaeus, 'Your faith has healed you' – a phrase he uses throughout the Gospels – and sometimes even rebukes people for their unbelief. On one occasion he makes a startling promise: 'If you have faith as small as a mustard seed . . . Nothing will be impossible for you.'[18] The writer of Hebrews says that 'without faith it is impossible to please God'.[19]

This is a weird moment in world history to be thinking about faith. We are simultaneously both cynical and gullible, fearful of missing out, yet afraid of commitment too. At such a time, how do we become less jaded and guarded, more faith-filled and expectant, without kissing our brains goodbye? There is much I could say here, and I would seriously encourage you to conduct your own Bible study on this important subject, but for now let me assure you that the gift of greater faith is no less available to you than it was to George Müller, first in the *person* of Christ, and second in the *practice* of trust.

Finding faith in the person of Christ

Faith is found in *the person of Christ*. If you lack faith it's futile trying to stir it up from within. You can't fake it or make it materialise by clenching your buttocks and trying to believe three impossible things before breakfast. If you want to trust Jesus more, get to know him more. Look at him more, listen to him more, spend more time with him. It really is that simple. The more you see Jesus, the more you will trust him, because he's the most reliable, loving and powerful person you will ever meet. Fix your eyes on Jesus, urges the writer of Hebrews, because he is 'the pioneer and perfecter of faith'.[20] His job is to perfect your imperfect faith. Yours is just to stay focused on him.

Hudson Taylor, the great apostle to China, said that 'the issue is not greater faith, but faith in a great God'.[21] He was right! Don't focus on faith, focus on God. It's as you spend time focusing on his greatness in worship, remembering his kindness and rejoicing in his faithfulness, that your faith quotient will rise. It's by celebrating the small things that God has already done that you'll find faith for the things he hasn't done yet. Record answers to prayer and return to them regularly. Absorb God's words in the Bible (especially his promises). Invest time with those who are contagiously full of his Spirit. Avoid those whose cynical attitudes sap your spiritual strength. Do these things regularly and your faith will grow.

Finding faith in the practice of trust

The second way to grow in faith is *by practising trust*. I say practising because that's exactly what it takes: practice, repetition,

neural realignment, accumulated muscle-memory. Faith has
often been described in precisely these terms: as a muscle that
gets stronger with regular exercise. I know this is true in my
own life. At the start of the 24–7 movement we had nothing:
no money, no staff, no clue how to do what the Lord was asking
of us. We didn't even have a computer, so I prayed for one. It
seemed such a preposterous prayer, but God duly provided us
with a PC (sadly not a Mac) and we were so excited. I still
remember the thrill of lifting that enormous beige monitor out
of its box! God continued to answer our prayers and I found
that my faith in his faithfulness became stronger. Now that we
have many computers – and yes, some of them are even Macs
– I seem to be able to trust God for sums of money that would
have terrified me back at the start. I think my faith muscles
must have grown through regular exercise!

GOD'S 'SUDDENLY' HAPPENS SLOWLY. MOST INSTANT MIRACLES TAKE YEARS

George Müller exercised faith on an industrial scale for thousands of vulnerable people, and he certainly saw extraordinary
answers to prayer, but he also endured hardships. Many of his
prayers weren't answered dramatically. Others weren't answered
at all. Müller was a man of faith, for sure, but he was also a
man of faithfulness who endured discouragement and refused
to stop asking.

Have you ever noticed the way that little children ask their
parents for a thing again and again? They persist. They pester.
They nag! In a way they are learning to intercede. Jesus warned
us very specifically that we will sometimes have to 'keep praying
and not give up', telling a parable about a persistent widow
who kept hassling an uncaring judge until she received her
reward.[22] Elsewhere, he told his disciples to ask, seek and knock,
and, in the original Greek, these verbs were written in the
present active imperative tense, which means that they literally
mean: 'Keep on asking, and you will receive . . . Keep on seeking,

and you will find. Keep on knocking, and the door will be opened to you.'[23] There is a sense of habit, of repetition, of a reward for prayerful perseverance.

Faith is God's gift to us, faithfulness is ours to him. God's 'suddenly' happens slowly. Most instant miracles take years. Study them carefully and you'll discover that they owe far less to faith in that one dramatic moment than they do to years of faithful endurance behind the scenes, quietly asking, waiting and trusting. It's impossible to grow in faith without growing in faithfulness, and it's impossible to grow in faithfulness if all your prayers are answered right away. But when we endure delays, disappointments and discouragements without giving up or backing down – when we keep 'beating on heaven's door with bruised knuckles in the dark', as George Buttrick described it – our faith expands into faithfulness.

Traffic lights

Of course, some of your prayers will not require perseverance. They will be answered the moment you ask. You'll get an immediate *green light* from God! Others won't ever be answered, no matter how long you persevere. They'll be met with a *red light* and this may be deeply painful and perplexing (more on this in Chapter 7). But there are other prayers – perhaps even the majority – that get neither an immediate 'yes', nor a firm 'no'. They are *amber lights* requiring us to wait and persevere.

The great preacher D.L. Moody died fifteen years before the invention of traffic lights, so he wouldn't have understood this analogy, but he certainly knew all about waiting and persevering in prayer. In fact, he carried a list of one hundred non-Christians for whom he prayed daily. Over the years, whenever one of them gave their life to Christ, Moody would cross their name off the list so that, by the time of his death, no fewer than 96 of those 100 people had become followers of Jesus. What an amazing testimony to the power of perseverance. Even more remarkably, the remaining four surrendered their lives to Christ at Moody's funeral. All one hundred saved, simply because of Moody's

bloody-minded determination, his refusal to relent over weeks and
months and years. (See Tool-shed: *How to Maintain a Prayer List*.)

If an angel turned up tonight to say that your very next
prayer will be answered, I suspect that you'd be on your knees
in a flash! But how would you respond if that same angel told
you to pray daily, promising an answer on the 365th time of
asking? Would you do it? Probably! The truth is that none of
us knows how long it will take for a particular prayer to be
answered. It might take the rest of our lives, as it did for the
last four on Moody's list. But this we know for sure: that Jesus
has told us to persevere in prayer, not to abandon our cars at
every amber light; to keep revving the engine, faithfully asking
until his answer finally comes.

*   *   *

In this chapter, we have explored a number of key principles
for petitionary prayer, such as partnership and perseverance,
the importance of praying 'in the name of Jesus', and how to
grow in both faith and faithfulness. In the next chapter, we
will apply these same principles to the bigger horizon of intercessory prayer. How do we stand in the gap between heaven
and earth, praying on behalf of other people, other places and
even other nations, 'Let your kingdom come'?

MORE ON PETITIONARY PRAYER:

- **PRAYER COURSE SESSION**: #3: Petition.

- **PRAYER TOOLS**: 1. Palms up, Palms Down. 2. How to
  Maintain a Prayer List. 3. How to Pray the Promises of
  God (prayercourse.org).

- **FURTHER READING**: *J. Hudson Taylor: A Man in
  Christ*, by Roger Steer.

HERO OF PETITION:

Corrie Ten Boom: *Petitions in hell*

Is prayer your steering wheel or your spare tyre? (Cornelia 'Corrie' ten Boom)

Corrie ten Boom's family helped Dutch Jews escape the Nazi Holocaust during the Second World War. They were eventually caught and Corrie was sent to Ravensbrück concentration camp with her sister Betsie, who eventually died there. She endured unimaginable horrors, yet Corrie's life was marked by an unshakable trust in her heavenly Father, and punctuated by prayer. She seems to have lived in an almost continual conversation with God, asking and trusting her heavenly Father for everything. 'Any concern too small to be turned into a prayer', she said, 'is too small to be made into a burden.'

Praying in this way, the two sisters managed to live with extraordinary joy, until the day that they were transferred to a dormitory infested with fleas. Finally they began to despair. What possible purpose could their loving Father have in allowing their dire conditions to get even worse? But then, noticing that the brutal camp guards refused to enter their new quarters for fear of the fleas, they realised that God had used the fleas to provide them with a safe place for ministering to other prisoners undisturbed. Somehow those two indomitable sisters even began thanking their Father in heaven for the fleas.

When I hear stories like this I am ashamed to admit how often I fail to trust because I think God has let me down, or to worship because I don't feel like it. How quickly I complain about life's hardships while taking God's manifold blessings entirely for granted. Corrie and Betsie ten Boom's ability to worship in all circumstances reveals how deeply they had absorbed the first eight words of the Lord's Prayer. They were sure enough of God's Fatherhood to find evidence of his love wherever they looked. And so confident in his holiness, that they trusted in his ultimate control of everything from fascists to fleas.

Several years after the war, Corrie ten Boom was speaking about her experiences in Munich, when one of her former S.S. guards approached her at the end of the church service. '"How grateful I am for your message, Fraulein," he said. "To think that, as you say, He has washed my sins away!" His hand was thrust out to shake mine. And I, who had preached so often the need to forgive, kept my hand at my side.

'Even as the angry, vengeful thoughts boiled through me, I saw the sin of them. Jesus Christ had died for this man; was I going to ask for more? "Lord Jesus, I prayed, forgive me and help me to forgive him." I tried to smile, I struggled to raise my hand. I could not. I felt nothing, not the slightest spark of warmth or charity. And so again I breathed a silent prayer. "Jesus," I prayed, "I cannot forgive him. Give me Your forgiveness."

As I took his hand the most incredible thing happened. From my shoulder along my arm and through my hand a current seemed to pass from me to him, while into my heart sprang a love for this stranger that almost overwhelmed me. And so I discovered that it is not on our forgiveness any more than on our goodness that the world's healing hinges, but on His. When He tells us to love our enemies, He gives, along with the command, the love itself.'

6: Intercession

How to ask God for others

'Your kingdom come.'

---

*History belongs to the intercessors, who believe the future
into being . . . By means of our intercessions we veritably
cast fire upon the earth and trumpet the future into being.*
(Walter Wink)[1]

It is an article of Christian faith, and a consistent theme of
universal Christian experience, that sicknesses can sometimes
be healed, curses broken, churches revived, communities shaped,
catastrophes prevented, governments redirected and the future
formed, by the simple power of intercessory prayer. All too
easily my prayers can mostly be about me, but intercession
requires my centre of gravity to shift away from my own
personal needs towards those of others. In the words of Richard
Foster, 'If we truly love people, we will desire for them far more
than it is within our power to give them, and this will lead us
to prayer. Intercession is a way of loving others.'[2]

* * *

In a small Texas town, a bar-owner applied for permission to
extend his premises, but members of the local Baptist church
were staunchly opposed to his plans and launched a vociferous
campaign with protests, press-releases, petitions and even
prayer meetings. Planning permission was granted, however,
and building work duly began. The Christians felt bitterly

disappointed until the week before the grand opening, when a lightning bolt struck the bar and burned it to the ground.

The church folk were beside themselves with joy. Their prayers had been answered! Their cause had been vindicated! And so the furious bar-owner decided to sue the church on the grounds that it was 'ultimately responsible for the material demise of his livelihood, whether through direct or indirect actions or means'. Suddenly everyone changed their tune pretty quickly. All those who'd been trumpeting a miracle days before now rose up as one to deny all culpability. The case made its way to court where a judge surveyed the brief. 'I don't know how I'm going to decide this,' he sighed. 'We appear to have a publican who believes passionately in the power of prayer, and an entire congregation that has lost its faith entirely.'[3]

Intercessory prayer can be confusing at the best of times! Secretly we wonder whether our little prayers can make any actual difference in the face of vast intractable problems, like a relative who is entirely resistant to the gospel, or a terminal diagnosis, or a government that is oppressing its citizens, or the tragedy of a natural disaster. Our whispered prayers can seem feeble, foolish and futile against the sheer scale of life's troubles – a butterfly confronting a cliff.

And yet the Bible teaches that our prayers are vastly powerful. That's why, in the Lord's Prayer, Jesus doesn't just instruct us to pray personally for daily bread, but also for regime change: the coming of God's kingdom on earth. Elsewhere, the Apostle Paul urges us to intercede 'for kings and all those in authority'.[4] And in the Old Testament, God makes an astounding promise regarding the importance of prayer at times of national disaster: 'If my people, who are called by my name, will humble them-selves and pray and seek my face and turn from their wicked ways, then I will hear from heaven, and I will forgive their sin and will heal their land.'[5] The forgiveness of sins and the healing of the land are entirely contingent upon the intercession of God's people. What task could possibly be more important, more urgent for our world today?

One of the most dramatic illustrations of the power of such intercession comes in the life of that great intercessor Moses. When the Amalekites attacked the people of Israel he ordered Joshua to lead the fight while he climbed a hill overlooking the battlefield and raised his hands in prayer for victory.

> As long as Moses held up his hands, the Israelites were winning, but whenever he lowered his hands, the Amalekites were winning . . . Aaron and Hur held his hands up – one on one side, one on the other – so that his hands remained steady till sunset. So Joshua overcame the Amalekite army with the sword.[6]

This story models the spiritual warfare that rages behind life's physical battles (more on this in Chapter 11). Maybe the Apostle Paul was recalling it when he wrote: 'Our struggle is not against flesh and blood but against the rulers, against the authorities, against the powers of this dark world and against the spiritual forces of evil in the heavenly realms.'[7]

Perhaps this all sounds a bit ethereal but it is also extremely earthy and even ordinary. Talk to any Christian for long enough and they'll have a story to tell of a time when their prayers made a dramatic difference in the life of another person. For instance, just a few days ago I heard from Jonathan, a member of our church who works in London and arrived very early for a meeting in Westminster one morning in August. As he walked across the River Thames on Westminster Bridge towards the Houses of Parliament with two and a half hours to kill, he found himself thinking back to the terror attack that had taken place there the previous year. As he did so, he sensed a new and imminent danger so powerfully that he began to pray for protection (not something he would usually do), and continued pacing those streets and praying for an hour.

'It was so strange and so strong,' he recalls. 'I walked and prayed around that area praying for the safety of those who work in Parliament and the offices nearby, the hospital over the bridge, and the crowds of commuters. Eventually, around

7:30 a.m., I stopped praying and stepped into a coffee shop near the bridge. It was just seven minutes later and one hundred yards from where I was sitting that a terrorist drove his car into cyclists and pedestrians in the precise place where I'd been praying between Westminster Bridge and Parliament.'

We will never know for sure, this side of eternity, what difference Jonathan's prayers made that day. But what we do know is that the attack on Westminster Bridge the previous year left fifty people injured and five dead, but this incident killed no one and left three people with only minor injuries.

INTERCESSORS ARE THOSE WHO 'STAND BEFORE GOD IN THE GAP ON BEHALF OF THE LAND'

Those three injured people received assistance within seconds of the attack because the vehicle immediately behind the terrorist's car just happened to be an ambulance. What's more, CCTV footage revealed that the terrorist had been driving round and round these very streets in the hour before the attack, as Jonathan had been walking them, sensing danger, praying for protection against precisely this kind of attack. And there's one more remarkable 'coincidence' – Jonathan's wife Linda had woken unusually early that morning (something she would never normally do) with an urge to pray for him on his walk to work. It was strange because he commutes to work every day in another part of London, and she'd forgotten he had anything special on that day.

The Bible describes Joshua overcoming a direct enemy attack while Moses, supported by Aaron and Hur, prayed for victory. Perhaps on that day in London something a little similar took place when an ordinary commuter's prayers, supernaturally prompted, seem to have been used to neutralise impending evil, with the support of his praying wife at home.

Mind the gap

To clasp the hands in prayer is the beginning of an uprising against the disorder of the world. (Karl Barth)[8]

Users of the London Underground will be familiar with the phrase 'Mind the gap'. These three words, painted along the edge of curved platforms, are announced whenever a train arrives at many stations. To intercede is to 'mind the gap' between heaven and earth or, as the dictionary puts it, to 'intervene or mediate between two parties as the equal friend of both'. At the time of Ezekiel, God searched in vain for someone to '*stand before me in the gap* on behalf of the land so that I would not have to destroy it'.[9] Intercessors are those who 'stand before God in the gap on behalf of the land'. They mediate between heaven and earth as equal friends of both, pleading with God on behalf of people, and with people on behalf of God.

We witness Moses minding the gap in this way when the people of Israel bowed down before a golden calf. God says to him, 'leave me alone so that my anger may burn against them and that I may destroy them', but Moses says no. He refuses to back off. He doesn't roll over and say, 'Oh well, I guess you know best. If that's really what you want, who am I to stand in your way?' Adamant and defiant, he pleads with God to change his mind: 'Turn from your fierce anger. Relent and do not bring disaster on your people.' And his defiance works! His intercession appears to change the very mind of God. His prayers rewrite history. 'Then the Lord relented.'[10] When we read this remarkable story in the light of Christ, we can see that God's heart had never been to destroy but to save, and that Moses' prayers in this moment foreshadow those of Jesus himself who 'lives to intercede'[11] on our behalf, with infinite love.

Moses and the golden calf may well seem a far cry from your everyday attempts at intercession, so let's bring things closer to home. Imagine a mother and father sitting down one day to tell their only daughter that they've decided to divorce.

For that little girl, everything certain and stable – everything that has made her – is suddenly threatening to fragment. Solemnly, in a half-whisper, her mum explains that she's fallen in love with another man. Her dad is weeping. 'What about me?' the little girl cries. 'Where will I live?' Gently her parents ask what she would like. 'What I would like,' she screams, 'is for us to be a family.' She grabs her mother with one hand, and reaches out for her father with the other, trying with all her strength to draw them together. 'Mummy,' she sobs, 'just say sorry to Daddy.' Wild-eyed she turns to her father: 'Daddy, just forgive Mummy.' And so, here she stands in the middle, unable to take sides, belonging to both, pleading with every fibre of her being for one to repent and the other to relent, interceding for reconciliation.

This is the very heart of intercession. We may not always experience such extremes of emotion, but we do all inhabit the liminal space between heaven and earth, Creator and creation, glory and the dirt. Belonging to both we are unable or unwilling to take sides but long for them both to be reconciled.

Please don't take this analogy too far, however. I'm not suggesting that God is perpetually angry, continually demanding that we placate him in prayer. That would be ghastly. In fact, the most famous verse in the Bible assures us that 'God so loved the world that he gave his one and only Son' not 'to condemn the world, but to save the world through him'.[12] Having died on the cross he 'was raised to life – is at the right hand of God and is also interceding for us'.[13] In his death on the cross and now in heaven, Jesus is the ultimate intercessor. So is the Holy Spirit who 'intercedes for us through wordless groans'.[14] Here we have a remarkable insight into heaven as a place of loud intercession. To be 'in Christ' is to be drawn up into his intercession for the world. To be filled with the Spirit is to be filled with an interceding spirit. Where once we could ignore the problems of others, we begin to care deeply. We are sensitised to the world's brokenness. We yearn for our friends to know Jesus. Our lives take the shape of a single prayer: 'Let your kingdom come.'

Karl Barth, probably the greatest theologian of modern times, said that when we intercede 'we are set at God's side and lifted up to him and therefore to the place where decisions are made in the affairs of his government'.[15] Isn't that astounding? Imagine how shocked you would be if the president or the prime minister called to say that your name had been selected at random from a list of the entire electorate to spend a day sharing your insights on a range of issues with his executive, in the interests of greater democracy. I'm pretty sure you'd find the time to go. In fact, you'd probably cancel anything to attend. It might be one of the greatest honours of your life.

As a Christian you have already received an even greater invitation. The King of kings requests your presence 'at the very seat of government'. He offers you a permanent place on his executive so that you can influence his actions on behalf of nations. It is an unspeakable honour, yet we are often too busy, too disbelieving, or too insecure, to accept the greatest invitation of our lives. As Oswald Chambers says, 'The real business of your life is intercessory prayer. Prayer does not fit us for the greater work; prayer is the greater work.'[16]

* * *

We have seen that intercession means minding the gap between heaven and earth and mediating on behalf of others, but perhaps it all sounds a bit daunting. So let me give you four simple steps to help you grow in this vital aspect of your calling:

1. Get informed.
2. Get inspired.
3. Get indignant.
4. Get in synch.

1. Get informed – *engaging with the facts*
Let us send men ahead to spy out the land. (Deut. 1:22)

The first step in intercessory prayer is to get informed. Do a little reconnaissance. Find out the facts of the problem you are wanting to address.

I remember watching a five-minute news report about a corrupt leader in the Middle East and feeling outraged. I began to pray that God would remove him from power. But when I talked to Christians from his nation, they informed me that they were praying the exact reverse! Yes, their president was corrupt, but he was also preserving a delicate balance of power that was allowing the gospel to flourish. The alternative to his corrupt leadership, they said, would be far worse. I was embarrassed that I had not paused to get properly informed.

There may well be particular people, places and situations that God has put on your heart. Getting informed about them might simply mean phoning a friend to ask, 'How can I pray for you today?' Or it might mean listening carefully to someone at work until you really understand their predicament beyond the office gossip of 'Oh, her marriage just hit the rocks,' or 'He's always skiving off with a migraine.' It might mean signing up for the newsletter of an NGO that works in an area you care about, or researching the needs of a nation that God has placed on your heart, or even visiting that nation so that facts can become faces and problems can become actual people in real places.[17]

(See Tool-shed: *How to Intercede for a Large-Scale Crisis.*)

2. Get inspired – *engaging with God's word*
That which God abundantly makes the subject of his promises, God's people should abundantly make the subject of their prayers. (Jonathan Edwards)[18]

Having been informed about the problems, the next step is to get inspired by the possibilities. What might happen if God's purposes for a particular person, place or situation started to come true?

Someone challenged me one day to pray more specifically for our two sons. 'You need to find out', they advised, 'why he created your boys in the first place; the calling he placed upon their lives when he knit them together in Sammy's womb; the prayers that he himself is praying for their lives. And then instead of telling God what you think he should do for them, you can just join in with his prayers, which is way easier and more effective.'

For me this was a radically new way of viewing things. It reminded me of a Bible verse: 'No matter how many promises God has made, they are "Yes" in Christ. And so through him the "Amen" is spoken by us to the glory of God.'[19] What might happen if I stopped trying to get God to say 'Amen' to my agenda for our boys in prayer, and started using my prayer times to say a big, fat 'Amen' to his promises for their lives instead?

And so I decided to spend some time asking God what he wanted, instead of telling him what I wanted. Up to this point my prayers had admittedly become a bit vague: 'Bless the boys at school today; keep them safe; give them a good night's sleep; may they know your love.' That kind of thing. I could imagine the Lord saying, 'Yes, fine, but what are you actually asking me to do for them?' And so I found certain promises in the Bible that seemed relevant to the gifts he has given them and the hopes we have nurtured for their lives, and I began to claim these for the boys quite specifically in prayer. It seemed like a good idea but I had no idea just how dramatic the results would be.

One of the words I began claiming for our sons came from Luke 2:52, where a beautiful thing is said of Jesus as a boy: he 'grew in wisdom and stature, and in favour with God and man.' I took this verse and began to pray that our boys would grow in *wisdom* – academically 'with man' but also spiritually 'with God'. That they would grow in *stature* – maturing physically and in spiritual authority too. That they would grow in *favour* – with their peers and teachers, but also with the Lord. My prayers were becoming less vague, more focused than they'd been before.

A couple of weeks later, a remarkable thing happened. The boys were tucked up in bed when one of them called out and

we found him sitting bolt upright in bed. 'I need God,' he said.
'I want to pray that prayer!' What a joy it was to kneel by his
bedside that night, as he surrendered his life to Jesus. Right
before our eyes, he was growing in wisdom, stature and favour.

And then, the following day, Sammy's sister called to say that
she'd had a vivid dream regarding this particular son. Knowing
nothing about the decision he'd just made, nor the verse I'd
recently begun claiming for his life, she described a man appearing
in our study to say that he had 'found favour with God'.

Sammy and I were awestruck. Within days of beginning to
ask for wisdom, stature and favour, one of our boys had given
his life to the Lord, and his aunt had received a dream, more
than forty miles away, on the very night he did so, in which
an angelic visitor confirmed that he had indeed found favour.

**BY IDENTIFYING RELEVANT PROMISES IN GOD'S
WORD AND FOCUSING THEM ON A PARTICULAR
PERSON, PLACE OR SITUATION, YOU CAN BE
SURE THAT YOU ARE INTERCEDING FOR
THEM IN LINE WITH GOD'S PURPOSES, AND
THEREFORE 'IN THE NAME OF JESUS'**

I have been hesitant to share this story, because parenting
is complicated and life certainly hasn't always been easy or
plain sailing since then. We waited years before telling our son
about his aunt's dream, and there are plenty of other promises
that have not yet been fulfilled. But I want you to understand
just how powerful it is when you stop praying your own prayers
based on your own inclinations, and start praying God's prayers
based on his plans instead! By identifying relevant promises
in God's word and focusing them on a particular person, place
or situation, you can be sure that you are interceding for them
in line with God's purposes, and therefore 'in the name of Jesus'.

This principle applies to any intercessory context. For
instance, before praying the obvious prayers for someone who

is sick, try asking God how he wants you to pray for them. You may be surprised by his reply! Or before interceding for the city in which you live, *get informed* by doing a little historical research to establish why God caused it to grow in the first place, and then *get inspired* by trying to identify his promises for its future. My city was once the home of Britain's Royal Mint – all the country's money was made in Guildford – and I believe that we still have a calling to create and release wealth to the nation. Guildford also grew up around a monastic settlement (our biggest shopping mall today is even called 'The Friary'). Having identified this redemptive root in our past, and received many prophetic words about being a House of Prayer for the nations, we are claiming it for the future of our city too, doing everything we can to call forth the prayers and activate the covenants of those faithful old monks.

(See Tool-shed: *How to Pray the Promises of God.*)

3. Get indignant – *engage with your heart*
Intercessory prayer is spiritual defiance of what is in the way of what God has promised. (Walter Wink)[20]

There's a strange thing that can happen when you really lay hold of God's promises and begin to see his intended future for a contested person or place: you start to feel indignant about the ways in which his purposes are currently being undermined and resisted. It seems outrageous! You move beyond the saying of nice prayers, to a place of spiritual contention, like Moses with his hands held aloft for hours on end, or Jacob wrestling all night for God's blessing.

One of the most surprising secrets of the Lord's Prayer is that its original Greek renders every verb – 'hallow', 'come', 'be done', 'give', 'forgive' and so on – in the imperative mood, which can be a forceful, assertive, commanding tone of entreaty.[21] The Bible scholar Darrell Johnson concludes that 'To pray the Lord's Prayer is to command – not to ask – but to command.'[22] We are to pray authoritatively, not as timid servants pleading with a master, but with a quality of confidence tempered with reverence appropriate to us as sons and daughters of a King.

When Martin Luther's friend Philipp Melanchthon fell gravely ill, Luther prayed to God with surprising audacity: 'I attacked him with his own weapons, quoting from Scripture all the promises that I could remember, that prayers should be granted, and said that he must grant my prayer, if I was henceforth to put faith in his promises.' Luther's tone is shocking, yet the Father granted his request.

The nineteenth-century Scottish theologian P.T. Forsyth argued that this kind of contending is essential in prayer: 'Lose the habit of wrestling and the hope of prevailing with God, make it mere walking with God in friendly talk: and, precious as that is, yet you tend to lose the reality of prayer at last. In principle you make it mere conversation instead of the soul's great action.'[23]

Neither P.T. Forsyth nor Martin Luther were advocating irreverence or unnecessary emotionalism in prayer, but they were testifying to that aspect of intercession which is militant, passionate and defiant. They understood that there is a time and a place to pray through tears, to groan with the Holy Spirit, to plead with God until your voice gives out, to lay hold of his promises and insist upon their fulfilment, to go without food, to vent righteous anger, to dig your heels into a particular situation of injustice and cry out with clenched fists, 'Lord, let your kingdom come'. (See Tool-shed: *How to Fast.*)

4. Get in synch – *engage with the saints*
Truly I tell you, that if two of you on earth agree about anything they ask for, it will be done for them by my Father in heaven. For where two or three gather in my name, there am I with them. (Matt. 18:19–20)

One of the keys to successful asking in prayer, according to Jesus, is agreement with other people. This is why we say *Amen* – 'So be it' – when we pray: it's a way of expressing our agreement.

And it's also why church prayer meetings and prayer rooms are so important. If everyone just prays on their own privately at home, it's not the same thing at all. There is a unique power vested in the united intercession of God's people.

We see this principle clearly in the powerful prayer meeting of Acts 4. Having been warned in no uncertain terms to stop preaching, Peter and John reported back to the church and immediately, 'When they heard this, they raised their voices together in prayer to God.' As a result, 'The place where they were meeting was shaken. And they were all filled with the Holy Spirit and spoke the word of God boldly.'[24]

The miracle of Dunkirk

One of the most dramatic examples of the power of united intercession in modern times took place in May 1940, as the Second World War was entering its darkest and most dangerous chapter. The Allied forces were trapped by the advancing Nazi forces with their backs to the sea at Dunkirk. The German High Command had announced that its troops were 'proceeding to annihilate the British Army', Winston Churchill was preparing to admit an unprecedented military catastrophe, and Allied generals were secretly anticipating the loss of a third of a million soldiers. In utter despair, King George VI took to the airwaves on 23 May 1940, calling the people of Great Britain to a National Day of Prayer the following Sunday, 26 May. Old black-and-white photographs show sombre crowds that Sunday, queuing to get into cathedrals, churches and chapels, an entire nation united in seeking God for national deliverance.

It was the very next day that the famous flotilla of some 860 vessels – mostly civilian craft – set out to cross the English Channel in a desperate, ramshackle attempt to rescue besieged Allied soldiers. Churchill hoped that as many as 30,000 men, 10 per cent of the beleaguered army, could be rescued.

By the time the ships reached France they were highly vulnerable to aerial attack. So too was the Allied army amassed like a sitting target on the beach at Dunkirk. But unseasonal storms blew up, battering the European mainland so violently that the Luftwaffe in that region was grounded, unable to attack. Meanwhile, Hitler had inexplicably ordered his ground forces to halt. For three days they didn't move. His generals were furious and military historians to this day are still baffled by this clear tactical error. And so, with the Luftwaffe grounded by an unexpected storm, and the German army restrained by its own commander, the Dunkirk evacuations were allowed to proceed largely undisrupted until the Luftwaffe resumed their attacks on 29 May.

On the Wednesday, three days after the National Day of Prayer, an extraordinary calm descended upon the English Channel, in sharp contrast to the storms of the previous day, precisely the benign conditions that the overloaded boats now needed as they sailed precariously back to England. By the time that the German army finally renewed its attack, over 338,000 men had been rescued, ten times the expected number, including 140,000 French, Belgian, Dutch and Polish soldiers.

No wonder the events of those remarkable days became known as 'the miracle of Dunkirk'. In his famous speech to Parliament on 4 June 1940 Churchill heralded 'a miracle of deliverance'. A second Day of Prayer was called, two weeks after the first one, to thank God for delivering a third of a million lives, confounding the plans of the enemy, and redirecting the entire trajectory of the Second World War.

We must be very careful indeed about claiming God's partisan support or overt blessing upon any one side in any theatre of war. But it is without doubt that a series of critical elements in the success of the Dunkirk evacuations lay so far beyond the hand of the Allied powers that they must either be labelled as luck on a quite extraordinary scale, or as answers to the unprecedented, concerted prayers of an entire nation which ascended to heaven on the day that it all began.

Exactly four years after the miracle of Dunkirk, soldiers were once again being shipped across the English Channel, but this time in the other direction to liberate Europe. With the war entering its final throes, King George VI summoned the nation for one last intercessory push: 'I desire solemnly to call my people to prayer', he wrote in a message printed in every British newspaper:

> I hope that throughout the present crisis of the liberation of Europe there may be offered up earnest, continuous and wide-spread prayer. If from every place of worship, from every home and factory, men and women of all ages and many races and occupations, prayers and intercessions rise, then, please God . . . the predictions of an ancient Psalm may be fulfilled: 'The Lord will give strength to his people: the Lord will give his people the blessing of peace.'

* * *

In this chapter we have studied the priority and power of intercessory prayer and advocated four practical steps: getting informed, getting inspired, getting indignant and getting in line with other Christians. This is exciting and important work, but what are we to do when our petitions and intercessions appear to go unanswered? In the next chapter we're going to take a long, hard look at the difficult questions we must ask and the disappointments we all experience, whenever our heart-cries to God seem to go unheeded.

MORE ON INTERCESSORY PRAYER:

- **PRAYER COURSE SESSION**: #3: Intercession.

- **PRAYER TOOLS**: 1. How to Host a Non-Boring Prayer Meeting. 2. How to Intercede for a Large-Scale Crisis. 3. Circle Prayer (prayercourse.org).

- **FURTHER READING**: *The Soul of Prayer*, by P.T. Forsyth.

HERO OF INTERCESSION:

Count Zinzendorf:
The noble Jesus freak

Count Nikolaus Ludwig Zinzendorf was born in 1700 into an aristocratic Austro-German family. He was to cast a long shadow across the eighteenth century as a social reformer, bishop, hymn-writer, globe-trotting father of the modern missions movement, architect of a number of towns in Europe and America, founder of a religious Order, benefactor behind the famous Moravian village at Herrnhut and – above all – a man of prayer. Scholar George Forell summed it up best when he described Zinzendorf as 'the noble Jesus freak'.[25]

On leaving Halle Academy aged sixteen, Zinzendorf handed his professor a list of seven praying societies he'd established during his time at the school – quite the intercessor even as a teenager!

At the age of twenty-two, when a ragtag band of refugees arrived on his estate at Berthelsdorf near Dresden, Zinzendorf permitted them to build a village on his land, which they called Herrnhut – 'The Lord's Watch'.

On 13 August 1727, Zinzendorf gathered the Herrnhutters in the church at Berthelsdorf, and challenged them to apologise to one another for the quarrelling that had come to mark their fledgling community. As they did so, the Holy Spirit was poured out upon them in an overwhelming way. Two weeks later, twenty-four men and twenty-four women, inspired by Leviticus 6:13 – 'the sacred fire was never permitted to go out on the altar' – covenanted together to pray continuously for one hour each through the day and night. And so began the prayer meeting that lasted non-stop, night and day, for over a hundred years. Zinzendorf later recalled the transformation that took place as a result: 'The whole place represented truly a visible habitation of God among men.'

After five years of 24–7 prayer, Zinzendorf began sending out missionaries. Herrnhut would become the first and greatest missions base of the eighteenth century. At enormous personal cost, the Moravians – fuelled by prayer – propelled the gospel out to many nations where the name of Jesus had never before been proclaimed. Every missionary who left Herrnhut would partner with a family, who promised to intercede for them and to support them financially. In this very practical way, intercession and mission worked hand in hand with extraordinary effect.

The life of Count Zinzendorf, 'the noble Jesus freak', boldly inspires us to a life of all-consuming love for Jesus and reminds us that the life of intercessory prayer not only changes us but truly changes the world.

> I have one passion. It is he, only he.
> (Zinzendorf)

7: Unanswered Prayer

How to deal with disappointment

'Your will be done'

So far in this book we've focused on the wonders of prayer – the peace of *centring* ourselves in Jesus, the joy of *adoring* 'our Father in heaven', the blessings of *asking* for 'our daily bread', and the world-shaking, history-making power of *intercession* for his 'kingdom come'. But prayer isn't always wonderful. Sometimes it disappoints us deeply.

I am writing this chapter remembering my friend and mentor Floyd who has lain in a coma for more than a year in South Africa, despite relentless, worldwide prayer. I am grieving the death of my friend Tom, who was diagnosed with cancer in July and died just before Christmas aged forty. Our passionate prayers for Tom simply didn't work, and there is no redemptive purpose apparent in a young dad being taken from his kids, no human agency we can easily blame.

These are my questions as I write, and you will have your own as you read. And so we must step now into the shadows of Gethsemane to acknowledge just how painful it can sometimes be to pray: 'Let your will be done.'[1]

* * *

Pulling up nervously one Sunday outside a large church in Florida, I was ushered inside for breakfast with the elderly founding pastor, and then out into an auditorium to teach the first service of the day about prayer. Eager to please, I gave them all my best material, but the congregation just stared back at me blankly, unmoved, uninterested and unimpressed. I was failing badly.

The worship pastor took me aside at the end of the first service. 'Great job out there man!'

'Um, thanks.'

'Look, I guess we owe you an explanation. A few years back the pastor's wife got cancer. The church rose up and prayed like never before. It was incredible. We had faith for her to be healed. There were prophetic words. Special prayer meetings. People fasted. The kids. The High Schoolers. And then . . .' – he was half whispering – 'and then she died.'

'I'm sorry,' I said. 'I didn't know.'

'Pastor took some compassionate leave. Returned to the pulpit. Started a new series. Life moved on like nothing had happened. But I guess we're all still hurting.' He looked me in the eyes for the first time. 'We're wondering why our prayers didn't work. How we explain it to our kids. Why those prophecies didn't come true. How we're ever supposed to trust God again in quite the same way. So, when someone like you turns up,' he flashed an apologetic grin, 'and you start talking about how powerful and wonderful prayer is, well forgive me but, we just kinda think . . .'

His voice trailed off. It all made sense. Here was a church with a broken heart and a hornet's nest of unanswered questions they didn't even dare to articulate. They were never going to be able to move forward in faith until they knew it was OK to admit their disappointments so that their doubts could be addressed.

You are probably reading this book with similar questions about prayer. Every miracle story I've shared so far, every mention I've made of the Father's great love, may have provoked a tiny, involuntary 'Yes, but . . .' within you. Perhaps, like that church in Florida, you barely dare to voice your doubts.

The unanswered prayers of Jesus
The Bible is way more honest about unanswered prayer than the Church. The Gospel writers make no attempt to hush up the fact that Jesus himself experienced disappointments in

prayer. On one occasion he prayed for a blind man who was only half healed. He could see people but they looked like trees, so Jesus – even Jesus – had to pray again. In the Garden of Gethsemane, he pleaded with his heavenly Father, 'Take this cup from me', but the Father said 'no'. On the cross he cried out, in the throes of complete abandonment, 'My God, My God, why have you forsaken me?' but the heavens remained silent. And there's at least one of his prayers that remains unanswered to this day. In his great High Priestly prayer, Jesus prayed for us, 'that they may be brought to complete unity',[2] but clearly, tragically, we remain bitterly divided. It's an extraordinary thought that Jesus himself sits at the right hand of the Father today, carrying the pain of unanswered prayer. Surely we can be honest, therefore, about our own frustrations and disappointments with God?

* * *

If you've read any of my other books you'll know that this chapter is deeply personal for me. The subject of unanswered prayer hits very close to home because my wife Sammy was diagnosed with a brain tumour just months after the beginning of the 24–7 Prayer movement, and weeks after the birth of our second son. In a matter of days I went from believing that my prayers could save the entire planet, to doubting that they could save my wife.

We are unspeakably grateful that Sammy survived, and acutely aware that many others are not so lucky. But she still suffers from a form of epilepsy that demands a brutal daily arsenal of anti-convulsant drugs that deplete her immune system and leave her perpetually exhausted. I'm not fishing for your sympathy. Everyone has their own set of struggles, and these just happen to be some of ours. But I do want you to understand how deeply I care and how much I have wrestled with the things set out in this chapter.

In the Garden of Gethsemane we witness Jesus suffering pain

at every possible level: physically, psychologically and spiritually. 'My soul is overwhelmed with sorrow to the point of death', he said, 'and being in anguish, he prayed more earnestly, and his sweat was like drops of blood.'³ Jesus was suffering from a rare medical condition called hematidrosis, in which capillaries around the sweat glands can rupture under extreme anxiety and stress. Here, then, is a man suffering unimaginable levels of distress. Whether your struggle with unanswered prayer relates to a physical illness, mental health, or a spiritual void in which God seems to have abandoned you, Jesus truly understands. He's gone ahead and shown how to endure disorientation and pain.

1. Choose to be vulnerable with your friends
He took Peter, James and John along with him, and he began to be deeply distressed and troubled . . . 'Stay here and keep watch.' (Mark 14:33–34)

Jesus needed his three best friends by his side in his darkest hour. He didn't try to put on a brave face. He didn't pretend to be OK. He chose to include them in his distress, and even asked them to watch over him in prayer. There is a strong temptation towards self-isolation when our souls are over-whelmed. We want to roll up like a hedgehog or hide away alone. But Jesus modelled the opposite: actively involving his friends, drawing them into his private grief and engaging their support in prayer.

2. Choose to push into prayer
And being in anguish, he prayed more earnestly. (Luke 22:44)

Having enlisted his friends, Jesus went 'a little farther, he fell with his face to the ground and prayed' (Matthew 26:39). The temptation to isolate ourselves from others in times of trouble can also apply to our relationship with God. Our friends are essential but insufficient. Our greatest need is to lay hold of the Lord in prayer. One clear word from the Father can bring

more clarity and comfort than a thousand words from friends.
I was in Hong Kong when I got the news that my dad had
suddenly died of a heart attack on a beach in England. In deep
shock, I stumbled to my little room, knelt down by my bed and
prayed Psalm 23 through tears. 'Yea, though I walk through the
valley of the shadow of death, I will fear no evil: for thou art
with me; thy rod and thy staff they comfort me.' Six thousand
miles from my friends and family, feeling utterly alone, I experienced the comfort of God's presence there in 'the valley of
the shadow of death'.

I find it absolutely remarkable that the Gospels let us listen
in on the actual prayer that Jesus prayed in his darkest hour:
'Abba Father, everything is possible for you. Take this cup from
me. Yet not what I will, but what you will.'[4] Unsurprisingly,
these words have a very great deal to teach us about how to
pray in difficult times.

3. '*Abba*, Father . . .' – hold on to God's love

When his soul was overwhelmed, Jesus resolutely anchored
himself in the Father's love. His starting point in prayer was
'Abba, Father'. He didn't say, 'If you really cared for me you
wouldn't make me go through this.' The Father's love was
non-negotiable.

When our boys were very young and Sammy was extremely
unwell, I became their primary carer. It wasn't easy coping with
two children under three, the relentless demands of a growing
ministry, and the trauma of frequent trips to the hospital under
flashing lights. We were barely surviving and then, just when
I thought we had reached our lowest point, Danny contracted
chickenpox. Suddenly his perfect little baby body was covered
in itchy, prickly spots.

Watching Danny in such distress was horrible. I yearned to
tell him that it was going to be OK, that he wasn't going to feel
like this forever, that some people were even saying he would
have immunity in later life as a result. But, of course, a five-
month-old baby can't understand words, let alone concepts like

the progression of time and the science of viral immunity. All I could really do to soothe his distress was to bathe him and hold him close, waiting out the days and the interminable nights, as he screamed and scratched and cried himself to sleep in my arms.

When life hurts like hell and we find ourselves struggling to make sense of unanswered prayer, we may wonder why God doesn't just click his fingers and make everything better.

WE ARE PERFECTLY ABLE TO TRUST THAT WHICH WE CANNOT UNDERSTAND

At such times of unknowing, when there's nothing good in the pain, and we're helpless and hopeless as a baby with chickenpox, it's tempting to doubt God's kindness and to pull away from the Father's arms. But this is the very time that we need his comfort more than ever before.

It's important to remember that we are perfectly able to trust that which we cannot understand, '"For my thoughts are not your thoughts, neither are your ways my ways," declares the Lord.'[5] We may not be able to understand why God is allowing a situation to continue but, like Danny crying without comprehension in my arms, we can still choose to trust in the love of our Abba Father. His comfort comes to us through the support of others; through the words of reassurance and hope in the Bible; and through the solace of prayer. 'Do not be anxious about anything,' says the Apostle Paul, 'but in every situation, by prayer and petition, with thanksgiving, present your requests to God. And the peace of God, which transcends all under-standing, will guard your hearts and your minds in Christ Jesus.'[6] There is peace for those who pray.

4. 'Everything is possible for you' – hold out for God's power

Having addressed himself affectionately to God as Father, Jesus now unequivocally affirms his sovereignty: 'everything is possible for you'. If the first temptation when we suffer is to isolate ourselves from our friends, and the second is to question the Father's love, the third is to doubt his power. By downgrading our expectations in prayer, we attempt to protect ourselves from the heartache of dashed hopes. But Jesus doesn't do this. He clings to the Father's omnipotence even in his darkest hour.

No matter how hard it is to keep trusting when our deepest, most desperate prayers go unanswered, getting rid of God's love and God's power doesn't actually help. In fact, it makes things much worse. When you try to remove God from the equation of your suffering you reduce yourself to a highly evolved animal in a meaningless universe whose suffering is without purpose, consequence or hope. By holding onto God when things are tough, you retain the possibility of rescue and receive comfort in your distress, a sense of purpose in your pain, and ultimately the hope of life after death.

5. 'Take this cup from me' – be honest

Having affirmed both God's love ('Abba, Father'), and his power ('everything is possible for you'), Jesus prays five of the most surprising words in the entire Bible. He asks God for an alternative to the cross. This is Jesus at his most vulnerable, and he appears to be praying 'unbiblically'.

It's fascinating to note that Christ's prayer here in Gethsemane traces the form of his own Lord's Prayer almost exactly:

Our Father	Abba father,
in heaven, hallowed be your name.	everything is possible for you.
Your kingdom come,	Take this cup from me.
your will be done, on earth	Yet not what I will but
as it is in heaven	your will be done.

But while the first and third lines mirror the Lord's Prayer almost exactly, Jesus seems to go 'off script' in the second line. He flips it around, swapping 'your kingdom come', for the exact opposite, 'take this cup from me'. Jesus knows that the coming of this kingdom will mean drinking a cup of unbearable suffering, and he simply doesn't want to do it. The contrast between what he is *meant* to pray at this point, and what he actually does say, is startling. I imagine an audible gasp in heaven, tears in the Father's eyes as he watches his Son suffering and is tempted to relent. Here is Jesus fragile and off message, saying in effect, 'Abba, I'm scared. Help me! I don't want to suffer.'

Some people attempt to put on a brave face when they suffer. They pretend that everything's fine when in fact they're terrified and falling apart. Others try to manipulate God by playing religious games, saying the things they think he wants them to say. (Who hasn't tried to strike a deal – offering God all kinds of piety in exchange for the miracle we crave?) In the first chapter I wrote about the importance of radical honesty in prayer, and this becomes even more necessary when we are in any kind of pain. It's hard to overstate the extent to which these five words, at the heart of Christ's prayer in Gethsemane, have given permission to people ever since to pray imperfectly, honestly and even improperly at times of tribulation.

* * *

MOST UNANSWERED PRAYERS CAN BE ATTRIBUTED TO EITHER GOD'S WORLD, GOD'S WAR OR GOD'S WILL

By praying 'Abba Father' we affirm that he wants the best for us, and by adding 'everything is possible for you' we assert that he has the power to intervene. But, of course, if these two things are true – if God really is all-loving and all-powerful – why on earth does he permit so much needless suffering in his world? Why did he take my friend Tom from his children? Why is Floyd still lying in a coma? Why has he still not fully healed my wife? These are obviously vast and vital questions, which I attempt to address more fully elsewhere in my book *God on Mute*, but for now let me just suggest that most unanswered prayers can be attributed to either *God's world, God's war* or *God's will.*[7]

God's world

Let's start with the easy ones: some prayers aren't answered for fairly obvious reasons. For instance, if I'm standing on one side of a football stadium praying for my team to win, and another fan on the opposite side is praying for his team to win, who is God supposed to answer? And what sort of god would he be if he was constantly meddling in a zillion sporting events at the behest of anyone who happened to be praying? Isn't it obvious that he has established laws and principles in nature that make the world go round? If a Portsmouth FC player kicks a ball at the right speed, in the right direction, at the right time he will score a goal. If he doesn't, unfortunately he won't. My prayers are pretty much irrelevant.

God has intricately established certain governing principles that make the world work best for most people in most places most of the time. The majority of humanity does not experience devastating natural disasters. Most babies are born healthy. Fallen nature still contains far more beauty than ugliness. And so God tends not to tinker with these extraordinarily delicate, complex and effective rules every time we pray.[8]

I read somewhere that when Jimmy Carter was president he also ran the White House tennis rota. God does not run the White House tennis rota. He refuses to micromanage the universe. You simply don't find him tinkering with the laws of science every time a dissatisfied customer quotes a Bible verse in prayer.

THE CREATOR IS NOT A COSMIC SLOT MACHINE, WAITING TO OBLIGE OUR PRAYERS WITH A CAN OF COKE OR PEACE IN THE MIDDLE EAST

When you drop a brick on your toe, it hurts your toe. Yes, the Father loves you. Yes, he knows the number of hairs on your head and therefore presumably, by extension, also values the state of your toes. No, he doesn't want you to suffer unnecessary pain. But he will sit back and let gravity do its thing. Bricks do not hover above the feet of cherished believers.

The Creator is not a cosmic slot machine, waiting to oblige our prayers with a can of Coke or peace in the Middle East. Neither is he a mad inventor continually fiddling with his own inventions. And he certainly isn't one of those ghastly heli-copter parents, pouncing from the sky every time we might possibly make a mistake or get ourselves hurt. He is entirely relaxed about who plays who on the tennis courts next Thursday.

It's not that God's too busy with the world's problems to arrange tennis matches. One of the good things about being omnipotent, omniscient and omnipresent is presumably that you can knock up a tennis rota fairly easily while also keeping an eye on Kim Jong-un and attending the latest Hillsong confer-ence. But God has intricately designed the laws of science to work for the best for the majority most of the time. If every bride had a sunny wedding day, every farmer would be praying for rain.

The laws of science are explanations of the ways in which God mostly chooses to act, but sometimes he exercises his right to go off-piste. When Jesus turned water into wine he broke the laws of chemistry. When he walked on water, he defied the law of gravity. He even broke the Second Law of Thermodynamics by rising from the dead. C.S. Lewis says, 'That God can and does, on occasions, modify the behaviour of matter and produce what we call miracles is part of Christian faith', before he adds: 'But the very conception of a common, and therefore stable, world demands that these occasions should be extremely rare.'[9]

God's war

Your enemy the devil prowls around like a roaring lion looking for someone to devour. (1 Pet. 5:8)

Some prayers aren't answered because there is an active enemy at work in our world attacking and opposing the work of God – we live in a battle-zone. As Christians we are not immune from collateral damage and we are often targets. Jesus instructs us to pray therefore, 'Let your will be done on earth as it is in heaven', because it is neither a current reality nor an immediate inevitability. God doesn't always get his way even though he is God. When a child is trafficked, or a woman is raped, this is not the will of God. This is manifest evil at work. We must therefore learn how to exercise spiritual authority in prayer, wielding 'the sword of the Spirit, which is the word of God'[10] against Satan's attacks, actively subverting his systems and strategies, accepting that while we will not win every battle in this life – there will be pain – the war will one day soon be won forever. There is much more to be said on this important subject of spiritual warfare, which I address in Chapter 11.

God's will

Having said that some prayers go unanswered because they oppose the laws of nature, and others because they are opposed by satanic powers, still others go unanswered because they are opposed not necessarily by nature, nor even by Satan, but by God himself. Remember that Jesus only ever promised to answer prayers aligned with his will and purpose.

Astronomers recently discovered seven planets perfectly orbiting a star some forty light-years from earth. The Hubble telescope has so far found 100 billion galaxies in the universe. Doesn't it stand to reason that the One who made and maintains this vast cosmos will sometimes do things we can't comprehend, and that he can be trusted with the patterns and the purpose of our own little lives? There are many unanswered prayers that I may never understand – Sammy's ongoing, unhealed epilepsy, Floyd's coma, Tom's sudden death, to name a few. But Jesus ultimately invites me to trust in his wisdom, love and power beyond my own limited capacity to understand, praying with him the hardest and most powerful prayer of all: 'not my will, but your will be done'.

6. 'Yet not what I will, but your will be done' – the prayer of relinquishment

In the extremes of agony and sweating blood, Jesus relinquishes control. He may not want God's will, but he chooses it nonetheless. There is an invitation here to a darker kind of trust. To surrender ourselves to the will of God, not just when it makes sense and feels good, but when it makes no sense at all and even hurts us deeply.

We read the Gethsemane prayer, with the benefit of hindsight, understanding exactly why Christ's prayers had to be unanswered. And the Bible assures us that one day we will look back on our own lives, just as we look back on Christ's life now, and at last we will understand why it was that the Father denied some of our most heartfelt requests. As P.T. Forsyth says, 'We shall come one day to a heaven where we shall gratefully know that God's great refusals were sometimes the true answers to our truest prayers.'[11]

I can't think of a better way to conclude this difficult chapter than with these wonderful words spoken of John Newton, the former slave-trader and author of the hymn 'Amazing Grace':

> Some Christians are called to endure a disproportionate amount of suffering. Such Christians are a spectacle of grace to the church, like flaming bushes unconsumed, and cause us to ask, like Moses: 'Why is this bush not burned up?' The strength and stability of these believers can be explained only by the miracle of God's sustaining grace. The God who sustains Christians in unceasing pain is the same God – with the same grace – who sustains me in my smaller sufferings. We marvel

at God's persevering grace and grow in our confidence in Him
as He governs our lives.[12]

A Prayer of Relinquishment

Lord, I do not know what to ask of you; only you know

    what I need. I simply present myself to you;

I open my heart to you;

I have no other desire than to accomplish your will.

    Teach me to pray.

Amen. (François Fénelon)

MORE ON UNANSWERED PRAYER:

- **PRAYER COURSE SESSION**: #5: Unanswered Prayer.

- **PRAYER TOOLS**: (1) The Prayer of Relinquishment.
  (2) How to Lament (prayercourse.org).

- **FURTHER READING**: *Luminous Dark,* by Alain
  Emmerson; *God on Mute,* by Pete Greig.

HERO OF UNANSWERED PRAYER:

Joni Eareckson Tada:
When the spotlight doesn't shine on you

He has chosen not to heal me, but to hold me.
The more intense the pain, the closer His embrace.
(Joni Eareckson Tada)

Joni Eareckson Tada was a fun-loving, active seventeen-year-old, enamoured by the world around her and charmed by the opportunities life held for her. She went to the beach one day in the summer of 1967 with her sister. Diving into the bay she misjudged the shallowness of the water and tragically broke her spine. For more than fifty years she has been paralysed from her shoulders down.

Joni cried out to God with complete faith for healing. 'I followed every scriptural injunction: I was anointed with oil, I went to the elders, I confessed sin. I would call my friends up on the telephone and insist, "Hey, the next time you're going to see me, I'm going to be on my feet. Have faith with me, believe with me."'[13]

But the healing she longed for didn't come, leading her into depression, battling suicidal thoughts and religious doubts. On one occasion, Joni attended a healing meeting. As she watched Katherine Kuhlman preach, and listened to people share testimonies of healing, she became aware of a spotlight centred on the corner of the ballroom where healings were taking place. Her heart began to race with hope-filled adrenaline. In her own haunting words, 'the spotlight switched to another corner, and I was getting more excited, thinking that maybe the spotlight will come and hit the wheelchair section. But it never did.' It never did! What to do when the spotlight doesn't shine on you? When it feels as though certain prayers never get answered – at least not the way you want them to be?

Joni's disability is the consequence of a fractured spine between the fourth and fifth cervical level vertebrae, having dived into shallow water at Chesapeake Bay. It wasn't a spiritual attack – it was not *God's war*. Her injuries are tragically consistent with the laws and principles of *God's world*. But why has he not healed her? Wouldn't that be an incredible testimony? I think Joni would say that it has been *God's will* to bring comfort, hope and advocacy to millions of people – many of them disabled – through her testimony of unhealing. She still believes that she'll throw another rock into the swamp one day, pray another prayer and walk out of her wheelchair healed, but it may not be this side of heaven. And so, in the meantime, she continues to pray Christ's painful prayer of relinquishment: 'Abba Father, everything is possible for you . . . yet not what I will, but your will be done.' After years of wrestling with God, Joni can somehow say, '*this paralysis is my greatest mercy*'.

'*God uses suffering to purge sin from our lives, strengthen our commitment to him, force us to depend on grace, bind us together with other believers, produce discernment, foster sensitivity, discipline our minds, spend our time wisely, stretch our hope, cause us to know Christ better, make us long for the truth, lead us to the repentance of sin, teach us to give thanks in times of sorrow, increase faith, and strengthen character.*'[14]

STEP 4: YIELD

Contemplation, Listening, Confession & Spiritual Warfare

I urge you, brothers and sisters, in view of God's mercy, to offer your bodies as a living sacrifice, holy and pleasing to God – this is your true and proper worship. (Rom. 12:1)

The deepest prayer at its nub is a perpetual surrender to God. (Thomas Merton)[1]

The final step in the dance of prayer is surrender. It's a clenched fist slowly opening; an athlete lowering himself into an ice-bath; a field of California poppies turning to the sun. We yield to God's presence 'on earth as it is in heaven' through *contemplative prayer* and by *listening* to his word which is 'our daily bread'. We yield to God's holiness through *confession* and *reconciliation*, praying 'forgive us our sins as we forgive others'. And we yield to his power in *spiritual warfare*, asking our Father to 'deliver us from evil'. And so, in all these ways, it's by surrendering to God that we overcome, by emptying ourselves that we are filled, and by yielding our lives in prayer that our lives themselves can become a prayer – the Lord's Prayer – in the end.

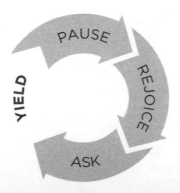

8. Contemplation

How to pray without words

'On earth as in heaven.'

You are here to kneel
Where prayer has been valid. And prayer is more
Than an order of words, the conscious occupation
Of the praying mind, or the sound of the voice praying.
(T.S. Eliot, *Little Gidding*)[1]

I was eating a Hawaiian pizza in an Italian restaurant with an old Franciscan priest called Brennan Manning. It was near the start of 24–7 Prayer and he was plying me with questions. We were using knives and forks, which isn't how pizza is meant to be eaten. 'So you guys are praying night and day?' I nodded. 'All the time?' I caught a mischievous twinkle in his eye. 'So tell me – how do you ever know when you've prayed *enough*?' I garbled an answer, trying to explain our model. How we were praying in shifts in dedicated rooms. Trying not to sound defensive. Trying to ignore his ill-concealed amusement.

The truth is that we were praying non-stop because we were desperate to see more people saved, more people healed, more miracles, the activation of hundreds of languishing prophecies. We were standing on tiptoe, trying with all our might to reach a big, red switch labelled 'REVIVAL'. Surely the whole point of night-and-day prayer was that it equalled the maximum amount of praying you could possibly do. This was the dial turned up to eleven, the secret sauce our mediocrity required.

The priest put down his fork and picked up a slice of pizza

in his hands, clearly more interested in it than anything I was saying. 'So would you like me to tell you how we see prayer in the contemplative tradition?' he asked. 'Please,' I said with a sigh.

'Say you spend sixty minutes in the prayer room. It's your quiet time, right? Your chance to read a bit of the Bible and check off your prayer list for the day?'

I nodded. An hour of prayer seemed pretty good to me. Frankly, I thought he should be impressed. None of us had ever dreamed we'd pray this much.

'Well, if that's really how you think prayer works, I guess you should consider your time in the prayer room as an hour off. The hour in the day you *don't* pray.'

'Wow,' I said, a little too enthusiastically. No clue what he meant. The priest sighed, pushed back his chair and stared at me. 'Look, what if you spent your hour in the prayer room just re-centring yourself on the Lord? Enjoying his presence. Listening to him in silence. Not bombarding him with words and lists and all that dutiful, earnest . . .' – he was waving his pizza around absent-mindedly – '. . . all that religious *activity*!'

Suddenly he reached across the table and patted my chest. 'You wanna know how God changes you *in here*, Pete? Silence! Contemplation! That's how you pray continually. It's like Mary sitting at Jesus' feet doing the one thing needed, while her sister is getting all hot and bothered in the kitchen.'

'I hear you,' I said slowly, and this time I meant it. 'I get it, but . . .' How honest could I be? 'But if we all just sit around listening to the silence, how will anything ever get done? What about intercession? What about the way the early church prayed? What about all the problems in the world?'

The priest took a sip of his Pepsi. 'I'm not against intercession and all those other kinds of prayer,' he said. 'In fact, I think they're essential. It's just that they're not enough. The world is so full of need. You watch the news and there's so much tragedy. How many things do you have to add to your prayer list after that? And then there are your friends: marriages breaking down, kids bullied, money worries, relatives dying. It's exhausting. It's overwhelming. There has to be another way. That's why I asked how you know when you've prayed enough. I wasn't being facetious.'

'And you think the way to address the world's problems is *silence*?' I countered.

'No. I think the way to address the world's problems is *presence*.'

I stared at him blankly.

'What if the hour you spend in the prayer room is when you refocus on Jesus so that you can carry his presence with you into the other twenty-three hours of the day with a heightened awareness that he is with you, he is for you, that he likes you, that he hears your thoughts? You start to pray in real-time. You instinctively lift situations to the Lord in the actual moment that you experience them – while you are watching that distressing news report, or hearing about your friend's latest crisis. You're no longer deferring all your prayers to some later, holier moment, because your whole life is becoming that holier moment.'

This was unfamiliar territory for someone raised in a tradition that tends to box prayer away in an all-important daily devotional, an optional weekly prayer meeting, and a ninety-minute service on Sunday. And yet it was alluring to think that there could be a deeper, more fulfilling way to pray around the clock, not just by saying a lot of prayers, but by *becoming* those prayers twenty-four hours a day. Not just by interceding occasionally for God's kingdom to come out there somewhere 'on earth as it is in heaven', but by becoming the patch of earth on which it touches down.

That conversation proved formative as the 24–7 movement grew, particularly when several of our key leaders hit hard times that provoked us to ask important questions about the nature of prayer and how it actually works. We began studying the lives of mystics and monastics like Anthony of the Desert in fourth-century Egypt, Teresa of Ávila in sixteenth-century Spain,

Amy Carmichael in nineteenth-century India, and Henri Nouwen in twentieth-century Canada. These people lived in different parts of the world, at different times in history, and came from different Christian traditions, but each one modelled the beauty of a contemplative life and its power to change the world by changing the person who prays. If petition is prayer at its simplest, and intercession is prayer at its most powerful, contemplation is prayer at its deepest and most personally transformational.

Stargazing and jazz

To turn from everything to one face, is to find oneself face to face with everything. (Elizabeth Bowen)[2]

Teresa of Ávila, the sixteenth-century Spanish nun whose book *The Interior Castle* is a classic on contemplative prayer, describes it as 'the prayer of quiet . . . an intimate sharing between friends'.[3] Canadian psychologist David Benner calls it a 'wordless, trusting openness to the God who dwells at the centre of our being, at the centre of the world'.[4] Richard Foster describes it as 'a loving attentiveness to God' in which 'talk recedes into the background, and feeling comes to the foreground'.[5] All such definitions circle the same three themes. First, that contemplative prayer is consumed with God's love. Second, that it is mostly a 'quiet', 'wordless' form of silent meditation upon Christ in which we just enjoy his presence without doing or saying anything. And third, that it is experiential rather than logical – 'an intimate sharing', 'a trusting openness', a 'feeling [that] comes to the foreground'. Contemplation is stargazing rather than astronomy,[6] listening to jazz rather than hearing a talk.

Some people worry that this might be a one-way highway to heresy, a dangerous gateway to New Age deception, and they are wise to be cautious. Contemplative prayer is powerful and highly subjective. We do need to remain discerning, biblical and radically focused on Jesus when we pray in this way. But it is the Bible that teaches us to do it. King David prays, 'May the . . . meditation of my heart be pleasing in your sight' (Ps. 19:14), and elsewhere he declares, 'For God alone my soul waits in silence' (Ps. 62:1, ESV). The Lord himself invites us to 'Be still, and know that I am God' (Ps. 46:10).

Jesus can't possibly have talked incessantly during those long nights he spent in prayer. He must surely have spent much of the time in silence, worshipping, meditating, listening and enjoying the Father's love. In other words, he must have prayed contemplatively.

When the Apostle Peter's prayer time opened out into a vision of non-kosher food descending from heaven and a voice saying 'Kill! Eat!' his theology was rewritten and the entire mission of the Church redefined. The Apostle Paul describes being 'caught up to paradise' where he 'heard inexpressible things, things that no one is permitted to tell'.[7] The Apostle John was 'in the Spirit' 'on the Lord's Day' when, 'I heard behind me a loud voice like a trumpet, which said: "Write on a scroll what you see and send it to the seven churches."'[8] And so the book of Revelation begins.

Such mystical experiences are not common, but neither are they rare. Some are ecstatic but most are less dramatic, yet all are legitimate expressions of contemplative prayer. Again and again the Bible describes encounters with God that are far bigger and more mysterious than the traditional expressions of petition and intercession. As T.S. Eliot says: 'Prayer is more than an order of words, the conscious occupation of the praying mind, or the sound of the voice praying.'[9] Followers of Jesus have every reason to expect and desire encounters with God in prayer that lie beyond the realm of language and logic.

We are commanded to love God with all of our hearts, all of our souls, and all of our minds, but most of us only use half of our minds – the left hemisphere of the cerebral cortex, to be precise – when we approach God in prayer. This is the area of the brain responsible for words and rational processing. The apostolic exhortation to 'pray continually'[10] is impossible unless we engage both halves of our brains in order to pray consciously

using words (left side), but also subconsciously by practising
God's presence when we're distracted or thinking about other
things (right side).

I'm aware that this could all sound a bit mystical and
unattainable. But I believe – quite passionately – that contemplative prayer is for everyone. In fact, I believe that most
ordinary Christians already practise contemplation and experience God's presence way more than they realise. Perhaps
you've known moments in corporate worship, when the lyrics
of a song seemed to recede, and time stood still. You found
yourself, in Charles Wesley's lovely phrase, 'lost in wonder,
love and praise'. Or maybe you've sometimes been sitting
alone quietly in prayer, or been walking outside, and God's
peace has gently enveloped you in a way that made words
seem unnecessary and even inappropriate. Perhaps you've
been filled with the Holy Spirit and received the gift of
tongues, and this has introduced you to the reality of a spirituality that is non-verbal, non-literal and experiential.[11] If we
will just start out with the things we already know and do,
we are all able to grow and go deeper in contemplative prayer
quite naturally and enjoyably. We shouldn't try to jump to
the top of the staircase in one go.

A shard of heaven's kaleidoscope
The experiential, non-verbal, right-hemisphere dimensions of
prayer actually come more naturally to many people than the
verbal, rational, mechanical varieties that we've been exploring
so far in this book. This is particularly true for children, and
those who find language cumbersome, such as people with
learning disabilities, or those with forms of dementia, not to
mention those who are exhausted, bewildered and burned out
on the brutal world of words and linear activity. Contemplative
prayer reassures us that it's OK to just show up in prayer. That
there doesn't have to be anything insincere about 'going through
the motions' when those motions express something we cannot
say in any other way. That some of the most beautiful prayers

in the world are children's pictures, the sighs of weary mothers, music that is unfettered by words.

THERE DOESN'T HAVE TO BE ANYTHING INSINCERE ABOUT 'GOING THROUGH THE MOTIONS' WHEN THOSE MOTIONS EXPRESS SOMETHING WE CANNOT SAY

On the second page of her award-winning memoir *Just Kids*, Patti Smith (the 'Godmother of Punk') describes learning to pray as a child:

> My mother taught me to pray; she taught me the prayer her mother taught her. *Now I lay me down to sleep, I pray the Lord my soul to keep.* At nightfall, I knelt before my little bed as she stood, with her ever-present cigarette, listening as I recited after her. I wished nothing more than to say my prayers . . . It pleased me to imagine a presence above us, in continual motion, like liquid stars.
>
> Not contented with my child's prayer, I soon petitioned my mother to let me make my own. I was relieved when I no longer had to repeat the words *If I should die before I wake, I pray the Lord my soul to take* and could say instead what was in my heart. Thus freed, I would lie in my bed by the coal stove vigorously mouthing long letters to God. I was not much of a sleeper and I must have vexed him with my endless vows, visions, and schemes. But as time passed I came to experience a different kind of prayer, a silent one, requiring more listening than speaking.
>
> My small torrent of words dissipated into an elaborate sense of expanding and receding. It was my entrance into the radiance of imagination . . . Lying deep within myself, the symmetry of a snowflake spinning above me, intensifying through my lids, I seized a most worthy souvenir, a shard of heaven's kaleidoscope.[12]

Patti Smith's progression from that depressing bedtime liturgy, via 'vigorously mouthing long letters to God', to the discovery of 'a different kind of prayer, a silent one, requiring more listening than speaking . . . a shard of heaven's kaleidoscope', is one of the best descriptions I've ever read of the contemplative progression.

How to practise contemplative prayer (and other cinematic experiences)

It may be helpful to think of contemplative prayer as a journey that passes through three clear stages, from meditation ('me and God'), to contemplation ('God and me'), to communion ('only God').[13]

1. *Meditation* – the 'me and God' stage

As it says in the very first sentence of the first Psalm: 'Blessed is the one who . . . meditates on his law day and night.' Contemplation begins with meditation – fixing your thoughts on a picture, an object, or most frequently on a phrase from the Bible. Sit quietly, reflecting on a verse, exploring it from every angle in your mind. Whenever you get distracted, bring your thoughts back to focus again on this simple, single phrase or sentence. Meditation is hard work, but it does get easier with practice. 'No other habit', says pastor Rick Warren, 'can do more to transform your life and make you more like Jesus than daily reflections on scripture.'[14] The poet Mary Oliver, who is known for her powerful meditations on nature, says that we have only to 'pay attention' to the wonder of the world – even its less beautiful bits – to step through the doorway into that contemplative 'silence in which another voice may speak'.

> *Praying –*
> *It doesn't have to be*
> *the blue iris, it could be*
> *weeds in a vacant lot, or a few*
> *small stones; just*
> *pay attention, then patch*

a few words together and don't try
to make them elaborate, this isn't
a contest but the doorway

into thanks, and a silence in which
another voice may speak.[15]

As we enter into contemplation through the gateway of meditation, we may well find that particular concerns begin to knock
at the door of our minds. When this happens, the contemplative
approach is neither to shut them out, nor to start interceding
about them, but simply to welcome them as guests and lift
them to the Lord in silent prayer. We acknowledge the situation
that is troubling our minds, or the person who is weighing on
our hearts, and lift them to the Lord. 'Intercessory prayer is not
primarily about thinking that I know what someone else needs
and trying to wrestle it from God', suggests Ruth Hayley Barton.
'Rather, it is being present to God on another's behalf, listening
for the prayer of the Holy Spirit that is already being prayed
for that person before the throne of grace, and being willing
to join God in that prayer.' Referring to the Apostle Paul's
description of the Holy Spirit interceding for us in groans
beyond human vocabulary, she continues: 'As I enter into the
stillness of true prayer, it is enough to experience my own
groaning about the situation or person I am concerned about
and to sense the Spirit's groaning on their behalf.'[16]

2. *Contemplation* – 'the God and me' stage
As I meditate on the Lord and become aware of his presence,
my centre of gravity shifts from 'me and God', to 'God and me'.
He takes centre stage. I'm no longer slogging away, trying to
fix my attention on him, using that logical left hemisphere of
my cerebral cortex, because I can now see that his attention is
already fixed on me! 'Just be there as simply and honestly as
you can manage,' teaches Jesus. 'The focus will shift from you
to God, and you will begin to sense his grace.'[17] As the focus

shifts from us to God, words become less necessary. Prayer is no longer something I'm 'doing', but something I'm *being* in the presence of God. 'The discovery at the heart of contemplation', says Bishop Stephen Verney, 'is not that I am contemplating the divine love, but that the divine love is contemplating me. He sees me. He accepts me.'[18]

3. *Communion* – the 'only God' stage

Sometimes it's possible to become so absorbed in God's reality that I forget myself completely. I am no longer consciously praying or worshipping. Words would be inadequate and even inappropriate. It's as though time has stopped and I've somehow stepped into eternity. An experience described by Anthony of the Desert more than 1700 years ago (in the observation previously cited) as 'Perfect prayer is not to know that you are praying.'[19]

You may be surprised to learn that you probably embark upon precisely this kind of meditative and contemplative journey every time you go to the cinema. First, at the start of a movie, it's 'you and the film'. You are eating popcorn, working hard to pay attention, tutting at anyone who's chatting, trying to get into those all-important opening scenes. But then, if the film is good, it starts to affect you. It draws you in. You laugh and cry. You find yourself caring about the characters, forgetting that they are actors. You no longer need to work at getting into the film because the film is getting into you. Meditation has turned into contemplation.

If a movie is better than good – if it is truly great – you will eventually get completely caught up in its plot, utterly absorbed and deeply affected. Your popcorn will be forgotten. It will no longer be 'me and the film', or even 'the film and me', but 'only the film'. The story will have transported you into a place that seems more real than reality.

Such all-consuming experiences and the overwhelming human desire for them – in art, in sex, in nature, in moments of sporting euphoria, in deep conversations with friends – are 'rumours of another world'. They whisper that we are made for eternity, wired to worship, happiest whenever we abandon ourselves to something greater and more beautiful than our own little lives.

Why contemplative prayer matters

We've seen *what* contemplative prayer is, and *how* to do it, but *why* should we really bother? Can't it just be filed away in the 'nice but not strictly necessary' box at the back of our brains?

Let me say this as clearly as I possibly can: your soul is crying out for a deeper encounter with Christ and, if your faith is to thrive for years to come, if it is to survive the coming seasons of darkness and pain, if you are to know and be known by Jesus in a richer, more fulfilling way, if you are to continue to engage with him when words no longer have meaning, if you are to become the loving person he wants you to be and to see the world the way he sees it, you must make space in your busy life for regular meditation, contemplation and communion with God.

'SHOW UP, SHUT UP, AND LOOK UP'

1. Contemplation as a way of being

'You are a mash-up of the things you let into your life', says Austin Kleon in his best-selling book, *Steal Like an Artist.*[20] If you mostly contemplate your phone, your neural pathways will realign to reflect that reality. If you fill your mind with pornographic imagery, you will become more (not less) sexually frustrated and lustful. Numerous scientific surveys have shown that if you surround yourself with people who are kind and speak positively, you will become more encouraging and optimistic. Children naturally and subconsciously pick up the accent and the mannerisms of their primary carer. And so, when we meditate regularly on God's goodness, and saturate our consciousness in his love, we become like him. In the words of Paul: 'We all, who with unveiled faces *contemplate* the Lord's glory, are being transformed into his image with ever-increasing glory.'[21] The more we gaze upon God's face in prayer as Moses did on the mountain, the more our lives will begin to reflect that very glory in the valley below.

My prayer life can easily become quite self-absorbed: a one-man echo-chamber of egotistical pleas. But when I pray contemplatively I have to 'show up, shut up, and look up'. It's far less selfish. And then, at other times, my prayers can become a bit utilitarian – a sequence of dry and dutiful intercessions on behalf of other people and places. When this happens, it is the contemplative impulse that draws me back to the place of grace and surrender, in which I simply 'waste time' with God, enjoying and returning his love unconditionally.

One of the most brilliant exponents of contemplative prayer in modern times was the Dutch priest Henri Nouwen. After a distinguished academic career holding professorships at Notre Dame, Yale and Harvard, he moved to a small community of adults with intellectual and developmental disabilities. It was a movement away from what he calls 'relevance', into the alternative contemplative way:

> These broken, wounded and completely unpretentious people forced me to let go of my relevant self – the self that can do things, show things, prove things, build things – and forced me to reclaim that unadorned self in which I am completely vulnerable, open to receive and give love regardless of any accomplishments. I am telling you all this because I am deeply convinced that the Christian leader of the future is called to be completely irrelevant and to stand in this world with nothing to offer but his or her vulnerable self. That is the way Jesus came to reveal God's love . . . Through contemplative prayer, we keep ourselves from being pulled from one urgent issue to another and from becoming strangers to our own and God's heart. Contemplative prayer keeps us home, rooted and safe, even when we are on the road, moving from place to place.[22]

2. Contemplation as a way of seeing

Contemplation changes us and it also therefore changes the way we see the world. Mother Teresa put it like this in her Nobel Lecture: 'We may be doing social work in the eyes of the people, but we are really contemplatives in the heart of the world. We are touching the Body of Christ twenty-four hours. We have twenty-four hours in his presence.'[23] To this day her order, the Missionaries of Charity, serve among the poorest people on earth as 'contemplatives in the heart of the world'. Their motive is ultimately not social work but worship, because they have learned to see the beauty of Jesus in the darkest places and to serve him in everyone they meet, most especially the poor. The great poet Gerard Manley Hopkins, a Jesuit priest, says something similar in one of his most famous poems:

> For Christ plays in ten thousand places,
> Lovely in limbs, and lovely in eyes not his
> To the Father through the features of men's faces.[24]

This is the contemplative gift – to see Christ not just in rarefied religious contexts but 'in ten thousand places . . . through the features of men's faces'. The more we see Christ in prayer, the more we see him everywhere we go and in everyone we meet. The whole of life becomes an invitation to worship.

* * *

Having opened this chapter with a story about a Franciscan priest called Brennan Manning, it seems fitting to conclude with one of his most poignant stories about a man called Dominique Voillaume, with whom he lived and ministered in a small uncloistered (open) monastery in Saint Remy, France.

> Dominique, a lean, muscular six feet, two inches, always wearing a navy blue beret, learned at age fifty-four that he was dying of inoperable cancer. With the community's permission he

moved to a poor neighbourhood in Paris and took a job as night watchman at a factory. Returning home every morning at 8:00 A.M. he would go directly to a little park across the street from where he lived and sit down on a wooden bench. Hanging around the park were marginal people – drifters, winos, 'has-beens,' dirty old men who ogled the girls passing by.

Dominique never criticized, scolded, or reprimanded them. He laughed, told stories, shared his candy, accepted them just as they were. From living so long out of the inner sanctuary he gave off a peace, a serene sense of self-possession and a hospitality of heart that caused cynical young men and defeated old men to gravitate toward him like bacon toward eggs. His simple witness lay in accepting others as they were without questions and allowing them to make themselves at home in his heart. Dominique was the most non-judgmental person I have ever known. He loved with the heart of Jesus Christ.

One day when the ragtag group of rejects asked him to talk about himself, Dominique gave them a thumbnail description of his life. Then he told them with quiet conviction that God loved them tenderly and stubbornly, that Jesus had come for rejects and outcasts just like themselves. His witness was credible because the Word was enfleshed on his bones. Later one old-timer said, 'The dirty jokes, vulgar language, and leering at girls just stopped.'

One morning Dominique failed to appear on his park bench. The men grew concerned. A few hours later, he was found dead on the floor of his cold-water flat. He died in the obscurity of a Parisian slum.

Dominique Voillaume never tried to impress anybody, never wondered if his life was useful or his witness meaningful. He never felt he had to do something great for God. He did keep a journal. It was found shortly after his death in the drawer of the nightstand by his bed. His last entry is one of the most astonishing things I have ever read:

All that is not the love of God has no meaning for me.
I can truthfully say that I have no interest in anything
but the love of God which is in Christ Jesus. If God wants
it to, my life will be useful through my word and witness.
If he wants it to, my life will bear fruit through my
prayers and sacrifices. But the usefulness of my life is
his concern, not mine. It would be indecent of me to
worry about that.

In Dominique Voillaume I saw the reality of a life lived entirely
for God and for others. After an all-night prayer vigil by his
friends, he was buried in an unadorned pine box in the backyard of the Little Brothers' house in Saint-Remy. A simple
wooden cross over his grave with the inscription 'Dominique
Voillaume, a witness to Jesus Christ' said it all. More than
seven thousand people gathered from all over Europe to attend
his funeral.[25]

The life and death of Dominique Voillaume testifies powerfully
to the beauty and purpose of the contemplative way. Through
years of gazing upon the Lord in silent prayer, he had been
'transformed into his image with ever-increasing glory' (2 Cor.
3:18). In Dominique's eyes this Paris slum had become a holy
place, not just a mission field but a sanctuary, populated with
broken people whose ordinary lives reminded him of Jesus
Christ.

He himself is my contemplation. He is my delight.
Him for His own sake I seek above me.
From Him Himself I feed within me.
He is the field in which I labour.
He is my cause. He is my effect.
He is my beginning. He is my end.
He is for me eternity.
(Isaac of Stella)[26]

MORE ON CONTEMPLATIVE PRAYER:

- **PRAYER COURSE SESSION**: #6: Contemplation.

- **PRAYER TOOLS**: 1. Silent Prayer. 2. How to Retreat for a Day. 3. How to Undertake a Pilgrimage (prayercourse.org).

- **FURTHER READING**: *The Sacred Year*, by Michael Yankoski.

HERO OF CONTEMPLATION:

Blaise Pascal: *Night of fire*

*The heart has its reasons which reason
knows nothing of . . .
We know the truth not only by the reason,
but by the heart.*
(Blaise Pascal, *Pensées*)[27]

Blaise Pascal was one of the greatest mathematicians, physicists and engineers of all time. While still in his teens he
invented the first mechanical calculator – a precursor to
modern computers. He created at least two new fields of
mathematical research. His Law of Probability is still used
by economists today. His name has been lent to a unit of
pressure and a programming language. He even developed
the first bus route for Paris. But the defining moment of
Pascal's life came on 23 November 1654 between 10.30 and
12.30 at night. Often described as his 'Night of Fire', we only
know about it because of some words written secretly on a
slip of paper and sewn into his jacket, discovered at last by
a curious servant after the great man's death:

Fire.
God of Abraham,
God of Isaac, God of Jacob,
not of philosophers and scholars. Certainty, certainty,
heartfelt joy, peace.
God of Jesus Christ.

That mysterious encounter with God changed Pascal's life.
Thereafter he turned his intellect towards theology and

philosophy. His book *Pensées* is widely considered a master-piece of prose. It includes Pascal's famous 'wager', which argues that it makes more sense to live as though God exists because if you are wrong your loss will be merely finite, and if you are right your gain will be immeasurable. But ultimately this brilliant intellect was not a rationalist but a mystic who argued that 'People almost invariably arrive at their beliefs not on the basis of proof but on the basis of what they find attractive' (*De l'art de persuader*).

9. Listening

How to hear God

'Give us this day our daily bread.'

A man prayed and at first he thought that prayer
was talking. But he became more and more quiet
until he realised that prayer is listening.
(Søren Kierkegaard)[1]

Prayer is a living conversation with a loving God, which means that we must listen as well as talk. In his book *The Universe Within*, Morton Hunt reports that babies born deaf make just as many noises as babies who can hear, but tragically their attempts at speech soon trail off. Everyone starts out in life trying to pray, but only those who learn to listen become fluent in its form. 'Just as a child learns to speak because his father speaks to him,' says Dietrich Bonhoeffer, 'so we learn to speak to God because God has spoken to us and speaks to us.'[2] But how does this work? Is it really possible to hear the Creator of the universe speaking personally to us? And if so, how on earth do we actually do it?

* * *

I was stranded in Chicago. All aeroplanes had been grounded by the eruption of an Icelandic volcano and I couldn't get home to England. I asked God how he wanted me to use the interruption. Several American friends had already been kind enough to invite me to stay but, as I prayed, I found myself thinking about a particular friend who lived 150 miles west in Madison,

Wisconsin. 'Hey, I'm in Chicago,' I emailed. 'Can I come crash on your couch?' I didn't know that Joe had just received terrible news, nor that his worried wife had asked, 'Who do you wish you had on your couch right now?' Those had been her exact words. Nor that he had replied, 'I wish Pete was on my couch, but I know that's crazy because he's in England and he's never even been to our home.' The prophet Malachi says that 'those who feared the Lord talked with each other, and the Lord listened and heard'.[3] Sometimes God listens to our casual conversations and receives them as prayers. Within hours of Joe's throw-away line, I had materialised upon his couch.

My friend Roger was driving along a busy dual carriageway. It was a hot summer's day and he had the window open, enjoying the breeze, until a sudden irrational compulsion provoked him to close it. Seconds later, an overtaking truck dropped a brick, which hit the glass where Roger's bare arm had been moments earlier.

Sammy and I had just moved to Guildford and we were talking with two other couples about buying a big house together. We had visited an amazing property and were excited about its possibilities for family, hospitality and mission. But an hour or two after the viewing I received a text message out of the blue from my friend Hanneli in South Africa, who knew nothing about our plans: 'I'm sensing that you are considering a new project – entering into some kind of new partnership – and the Lord says be careful. I don't think it's right.' Minutes later one of the others phoned me excitedly. 'So what did you think of the house, Pete? Shall we put in an offer?' Calmly but firmly I replied, 'No, I don't think it's right. I don't think God is in this.' With hindsight, it was a narrow escape for us all!

I was near the edge of burnout, trying to do three jobs – pastoring a growing church, leading an international ministry, and serving as Director of Prayer at a large Anglican church in London – alongside a full speaking schedule and trying to be a good dad and husband. I went on a two-day retreat, needing God to speak, desperate to know what to do, wondering

which of the three jobs I was supposed to quit. On the second
day I received a clear mental picture of a great, old sailing
ship crossing stormy seas at night. I was at its helm, trying
with all my strength to hold the vessel on course. And with
that image came four words: 'Hold your nerve, son.' That was
it. Clear as anything. Unexpected. Nothing else. It didn't help
in any practical way, and yet with God's word came a surge
of new strength, energy and resilience. I returned home
knowing that he had spoken, that I just had to hold on and
stay strong. Nothing had changed outwardly but everything
had changed within me. I couldn't do much about my overwhelming circumstances at that time, but God's word had
recalibrated my relationship with my circumstances completely.

SOMETIMES GOD LISTENS TO
OUR CASUAL CONVERSATIONS
AND RECEIVES THEM AS PRAYERS

God speaks!
My sheep listen to my voice; I know them, and they follow me. (John
10:27)

Each one of us can learn to recognise the voice of the Good
Shepherd for ourselves. What could possibly be more wonderful,
or more important than that? As we listen to him he dispatches
us on unexpected adventures, like my deployment to Joe's couch.
His wisdom instructs and guides us, sometimes stopping us from
making dumb decisions – like buying that big house. His Father
heart comforts and strengthens us when we don't know what to
do – like me battling burnout on that retreat. As the Psalmist says:
'Your word is a lamp for my feet, a light on my path' (Ps. 119:105).

But, of course, recognising the voice of the Good Shepherd
is not always easy. We've probably all been hurt by people who
misheard or misappropriated God's word. Others have endured
long, dry seasons in which he remained completely silent. How

then are we to discern God's voice with integrity, humility and a healthy dose of common sense?

* * *

At the age of seventeen, I gave up on Christianity. I had done badly in my exams, my girlfriend had finished with me, my friends had all gone away to university, and I was working as a toilet cleaner in a local hospital. Hurting and depressed, I needed God but he seemed a million miles away. I cried out and he didn't answer. I asked for advice, and he didn't say a word. I diligently read my Bible but nothing made sense. I dutifully went to church but everyone seemed fake. Either God wasn't there or he didn't care. So I quit.

A month or so later, a stranger approached me apologetically at the end of a concert and introduced himself as a Christian. He'd been staring, he said, at the back of my head for most of the gig, and kept seeing a random, recurring mental image of a flickering candle. The flame went out and everything went dark. But then it came back to life and lit up the whole room. That was it. Did it mean anything to me? Did it make any sense? Reluctantly, I nodded. The man just smiled and wandered off.

A couple of months later, I was shuffling through some Christmas cards when a Bible verse printed on one of them seemed to leap off the page: 'If you spend yourselves on behalf of the hungry . . . your light will rise in the darkness' (Isa. 58:10). I remembered the candle and knew, with absolute certainty, that this random Bible verse was for me.

A month after that I went to get advice from a wise lady called Nicole, and told her about quitting my faith, the flickering candle, and the verse from Isaiah 58. What did she think I should do? Nicole ran out of the room and came back with a letter from a missionary to Hong Kong called Jackie Pullinger. It had the whole of Isaiah 58 printed on it. Nicole told me to get the next flight and so it was there in Hong Kong that my

candle began to burn again. I was healed, changed, and commissioned to do the very things I've been doing ever since.

God had spoken. He had broken back into my life. But it
had taken the best part of a year and, at the time, it felt like
forever. He'd spoken to me in five different ways: through a
vision from a random stranger (to whom I owe everything), a
Bible verse printed on a Christmas card, a significant process
of personal reflection, the wise counsel of an older Christian,
and a willingness on my part to (eventually) obey. This isn't a
bad checklist of the various ways in which God speaks:

1. Hearing God in the Bible.
2. Hearing God in dreams and visions.
3. Hearing God in counsel and common sense.
4. Hearing God in personal reflection.
5. Hearing God in action.

1. Hearing God in the Bible

*'Son of man, eat this scroll I am giving you and fill your stomach
with it.' So I ate it, and it tasted as sweet as honey in my mouth.*
(Eze. 3:3)

When Jesus taught us to pray for 'our daily bread', he was
referring to physical provision (as we saw in Chapter 5), but
also to the daily spiritual nourishment of God's word. For
example, when Jesus was fasting in the wilderness and the devil
tempted him to make bread (the physical variety), Jesus replied
by quoting the book of Deuteronomy and pointing to another
kind of bread and another kind of hunger (the spiritual variety):
'It is written: Man shall not live on bread alone, but on every
word that comes from the mouth of God.'[4]

The Bible is our primary source of revelation, and the ultimate authority by which we weigh all other words. As the
Apostle Paul says, 'All Scripture is God-breathed and is useful
for teaching, rebuking, correcting and training in righteousness.'[5]
We verify prophecies, dreams, visions, angelic visitations,

premonitions, audible voices, supernatural hunches, and all manner of ephemeral inklings, against the absolute truths of Scripture. If they don't measure up, they don't get in the door. It's as simple as that.

But the Bible is more than an inspired doctrinal textbook. It is also 'living and powerful', as the writer of Hebrews says, 'a discerner of the thoughts and intents of the heart'.[6] In other words, while we are reading the Bible, it is reading us – discerning 'the thoughts and intents' of our hearts. We shouldn't just *learn* from the Bible, therefore; we should also *listen* to it. It's a totally different way of approaching the text: while learning about God *from* the Bible requires study, listening to God *through* the Bible requires prayerful meditation.

Pastor Mark Batterson says that 'scripture is God's way of initiating a conversation; prayer is our response. The paradigm shift happens when you realise that the Bible wasn't meant to be read through; the Bible was meant to be prayed through. And if you pray through it, you will never run out of things to talk about.'[7] How do we do this? How do we 'pray through' the Bible in the way Batterson recommends? First, try to read it slowly and preferably out loud. When particular words or phrases grab your attention, linger a little, savour them like a glass of wine or a favourite piece of music. Our educational systems and even our churches haven't taught us to read in this way – slowly and meditatively – but it's an exceptionally simple and powerful thing to do.

As you explore these phrases, personalise and apply them to your own life, allow your mind to go on bunny trails. Don't get too hung up on the literal meaning – this is a subjective exercise. Try to process the text intuitively the way you might view a great work of art. Or come at it like a cryptic crossword puzzle in which the words on the page are clues hiding a meaning and a message just for you. Try to turn your thoughts, your questions and even your distractions into prayers.

Let's try this approach with the most famous verse in the Bible: 'For God so loved the world that he gave his one and only Son, that whoever believes in him shall not perish but have eternal life' (John 3:16). Initially you might find yourself arrested by just those first six words: *'For God so loved the world'*. You could repeat them a few times, and feel the weight of that one little word, 'so'. God *'so'* loved the world. He didn't just love us a bit. He loved us a lot. It's extravagant. You picture the Apostle John underlining this word 'so' in the original scroll. You can imagine the Lord speaking your name, saying 'I love you *so* much'. Instinctively you reply, 'Thank you, Lord.' The conversation has begun.

LEARNING ABOUT GOD *FROM* THE BIBLE REQUIRES STUDY, LISTENING TO GOD *THROUGH* THE BIBLE REQUIRES PRAYERFUL MEDITATION

As you continue to circle these six words, you're struck by the fact that God loves 'the world' so much. Your mind turns to your own little patch of it and your annoying neighbour. You ask God to help you be a bit more loving today. You think of your friend Johnny. 'For God so loved Johnny that he gave Jesus.' You sigh involuntarily. 'Johnny doesn't want anything to do with you right now,' you say, sensing the deep sadness of it all. 'For God so loved Judith, lying there right now in that hospital bed.' You hadn't planned on praying for Judith. She just popped into your mind. Maybe the Holy Spirit is asking you to pray for her? You send her a quick text: 'How are you? Praying for you.'

I could go on. But we didn't even get past the first six words. Whenever we approach the Bible in this way, there are three internal shifts that begin to take place. *First*, we discover that there are prayer-prompts and conversation-starters scattered on almost every page of the Bible (even if the conversation some-times starts with 'Lord, help me to understand this bit'!). *Second*, our prayers shift away from our own personal priorities towards topics we might never otherwise have addressed. The Lord is setting his own agenda for our prayer times. *Third*, we hear him speaking to us more clearly as we stop reading the Bible and start praying it instead. (If you want to find out more about how to approach the Bible in this prayerful, meditative way, check out our Prayer Tool on the *Lectio Divina*.)

2. Hearing God in dreams and visions

Your sons and daughters will prophesy, your young men will see visions, your old men will dream dreams. (Acts 2:17)

Some Christians think that God only speaks through the Bible, but the Bible itself teaches that he speaks in other ways too! He speaks to us through dreams and visions, like that picture given to me of a flickering candle; he speaks through intuition, like Roger's impulse to wind up his car window; he speaks through prophecies and words of knowledge, like that caution texted to me from South Africa. He also speaks through creation (Ps. 19:1–2), through our consciences (1 Tim. 1:19), through angelic visitations (Matt. 1:20), through preaching (Rom. 10:14), and even on one occasion through a talking donkey (Num. 22:28)!

> ### I'M CONVINCED THAT THE MAIN GIFT GOD WANTS TO GIVE SOME CHRISTIANS IS COMMON SENSE

Someone in our church received a dream a few years ago of a rescue boat being pulled through the streets as people in the sea were drowning. It was a challenging image, but when one of our elders, Liz, had an almost identical dream a few days later, we knew for sure that God was speaking to us. In response to those two dreams we reviewed and redeployed our resources to prioritise reaching and rescuing the poor and the lost. A few weeks later, Liz and her husband Dave came to see me, sensing a call to work with 24–7 Prayer on the Spanish island of Ibiza.

I encouraged them to go and listen to the Lord in Ibiza and so, a few weeks later, they found themselves sitting in a restaurant in San Antonia, wondering if God was indeed sending them here. Suddenly there was a commotion outside and they watched in amazement as a rescue boat – the exact one Liz had seen in her dream – was pulled through the streets. Now they knew for sure that God was speaking to them, calling them to move with their family to the island to help rescue those who were drowning.

Of course, dreams, visions and prophecies are highly subjective, so we must weigh them against Scripture, apply common sense, and if they are directional we should also seek wise counsel. The Apostle Paul says that we 'prophesy in part' and advises therefore that prophecies should be 'weighed carefully'.[8] Mind you, he also urges us in the same chapter to 'eagerly desire' the gift of prophecy, so he is not in any way being dismissive. The Greek for 'eager desire' here is *zëloute*, from which we get words like zealous and jealous. I meet so many people who are merely, passively 'open' to prophecy, but the Apostle Paul says that we should be zealously, jealously desiring to hear God in this exciting way, because we long to bring encouragement, edification and revelation to others.

3. Hearing God in counsel and common sense
The way of fools seems right to them, but the wise listen to advice.
(Prov. 12:15)

I'm convinced that the main gift God wants to give some Christians is common sense. It is no less spiritual to seek godly counsel than to receive a supernatural dream or an angelic visitation, and it may well be far more helpful.

Seasons of listening and waiting for God's voice invariably conclude on either the Damascus road, with an unmistakable revelation of his will, or on the Emmaus road, with something far less dramatic. When God chooses *not* to speak in extraordinary ways – no angelic visitations or prophetic revelations are forthcoming – it's probably because he wants to speak in more ordinary ways, through conversations with friends, biblical reflection and the counsel of those we trust.

I remember going to see an old saint called Ishmael with a long and complex dilemma. Sammy and I were trying to hear God, reading our Bibles, asking for prophetic insight, and frankly not seeing eye to eye. I poured out my heart and he listened patiently for almost half an hour. When I finally finished he looked at me kindly and said, 'Pete me ol' son, you need to keep your wife 'appy.' With that he got up, put on his coat and left. I did what he said, put Sammy's wishes first, and realise now that it was absolutely the right thing to do. It was some of the simplest, sanest and most succinct advice I've ever received.

4. Hearing God in personal reflection
Mary treasured up all these things and pondered them in her heart.
(Luke 2:19)

Most people today miss the voice of God not because it's too strange but because it's too familiar. They expect the Almighty to sound dramatic, bombastic, unmistakable and a bit spooky. But when Elijah was hiding in a cave and experienced a 'great and powerful wind [that] tore the mountains apart', followed by an earthquake, and then a fire, we are told that the Lord was not in any of these great events. But then 'after the fire came a gentle whisper', and this was the voice of God.[9]

The 'gentle whisper' of God sometimes comes to me as an idea or a mental impression during a time of quiet prayer, but more often it comes afterwards, during a subsequent time of distraction. You've probably noticed how often some detail you'd forgotten – a person's name, where you left the car keys – suddenly pops into your head when you're no longer thinking about it later on. In a similar way, once you've asked the Lord to speak to you about a particular thing, it's often a good idea to stop trying too hard to hear him, and to occupy yourself instead with the kind of activity that engages you enough to be absorbing, but not too much, so that your mind has a little space to wander. This might be gardening, hoovering, walking the dog, or going for a run. Cognitive psychologists and neuroscientists explain that these sorts of activities switch the brain onto its 'default mode', a state in which we are better able to access our subconscious, connect disparate ideas and solve nagging problems. Periods of low-level boredom are essential for our psychological and spiritual wellbeing. Over-thinking is not productive. Intensity and earnestness rarely attract the Holy Spirit. We may well become more receptive to the whisper of God by occupying ourselves with less spiritual activities.

The Apostle Paul's craft as a tent-maker is generally portrayed by preachers rather dismissively, as if it were merely a means of making a living so that he could get on with the real business of proclaiming the gospel. In fact, the term 'tent-making' has become a euphemism for any money-making enterprise that funds 'ministry'. But the long, slow, laborious process of quietly making tents must also have afforded Paul the space he needed for contemplative reflection. It is highly likely that the extraordinary insights and exquisite turns of phrase that fill Paul's epistles actually came to him as he busied himself as an artisan making tents.

Since God's guidance can often come to me disguised as an ordinary thought or a whim, I tend to ask myself two questions before acting upon any such impulse:

1. *Is this like Jesus?* If I obeyed this idea, would the resulting action reflect the character and purpose of Christ? Is it the sort of thing he would do?
2. *What's the worst that could happen if I were to get this wrong?* If the answer is, 'Actually, it would be a disaster if I get this wrong', the red lights start flashing! I pause and pray. I ask advice from others. I take a little time to discern the best way forward. My general rule of thumb is to be wary of words that are harsh, heavy or directional.

When I was in Chicago stranded by that Icelandic volcano, I wasn't at all certain that my counter-intuitive idea of visiting Joe had come from the Lord. It was merely a fleeting thought that came to me as I prayed, but it passed my two criteria. Seeking out a friend and eating in his home seemed like the sort of thing Jesus would do. And, if God wasn't sending me to see Joe, it would hardly be the end of the world. So I decided to act on my hunch, pinged him an email, and discovered in doing so that my hunch had actually been the whisper of God.

In seeking to discern God's voice, journaling can be an invaluable tool for personal remembering and prayerful reflection. By recording our prayers and impressions in this way, we follow Mary's example who 'treasured up all these things and pondered them in her heart'.[10] The relative slowness and solitary nature of journaling ushers us into a more creative, less reactive state in which the hand of God is more easily discerned, and the whispers of his Spirit can often be more clearly heard. (See Tool-shed: *How to Journal.*)

5. Hearing God in action

Blessed . . . are those who hear the word of God and obey it. (Luke 11:28)

We often think of listening as a passive activity, but this is not the Hebrew mindset at all. Jesus said, 'You are my friends if you do what I command.' There is a direct link between obedience and revelation. In fact the Latin word *obedire*, from which we get 'obey', literally means to 'pay attention, give ear, or to listen'. Listening means yielding willingly to whatever God tells us to do.

Many people want God to reveal his entire master plan before they will commit, but generally he refuses to give anything more than the next couple of steps. When Mary the mother of Jesus told the servants at the wedding in Cana, 'Do whatever he tells you', it's highly unlikely that she knew exactly what her son was about to do. But she knew enough to trust him.

She understood that if the servants would simply serve, Jesus would somehow save the day. It's not until we have done the last thing God asked of us that we are ready to receive his next revelation. This keeps us close to his side, obedient to his voice, walking 'by faith, not by sight'.[11]

A number of years ago some dear friends of ours welcomed an unwanted, two-month-old baby into their home in Tulsa, Oklahoma. They noticed almost immediately that Anthony didn't cry, and that he had a flat spot on the side of his head where he'd been left sitting in his carrier unattended for long periods of time. Another worry was that Anthony's birth mother, Rhonda, had disappeared without completing all the necessary paperwork. Without this, Roger and Donna couldn't adopt the little boy, who had quickly become part of their family. In fact, he could still be taken away from them at any time.

They learned that Rhonda had left for Oklahoma City, one hundred miles south-west, without leaving a forwarding address. Not knowing what else to do, Roger printed a handful of fliers and drove off to Oklahoma City, hoping and praying that he could somehow find this one, transient woman – lost in the middle of one of America's biggest cities – among its 1.4 million residents. He knew it was crazy – a needle in a haystack – but they were running out of options and a child's wellbeing and entire destiny depended upon finding Rhonda before it was too late.

There's a verse in the Bible that says: 'Whether you turn to the right or to the left, your ears will hear a voice behind you, saying, "This is the way; walk in it."'[12] Roger entered the city that day, asking the Lord to guide him 'to the left or to the right' at every junction, every light, every street corner. Proceeding in this tenuous way, he happened upon a little white mission church in a dilapidated part of town surrounded by vacant lots. It was a Sunday morning and a service had clearly just ended because people were milling around outside, waiting for a hot meal. Roger parked his car and strolled apprehensively over to one of the cooks outside the church. She looked at his flier, shrugged, and suggested he talk to the pastor.

Recalling what happened next, Roger still laughs in amazement when he tells the story. 'The pastor looked at the picture, paused for a moment, and said words I could hardly believe. Yes, he recognised Rhonda! He knew her name. He even knew where she was living.'

'A sense of overwhelming relief swept over me. Of all the districts, streets, churches, houses and people in this vast, sprawling city, I'd somehow been led straight to the right man at the right address in the right neighbourhood at exactly the right time, just as the church was emptying. It had taken me less than thirty minutes to find Rhonda in the city that is America's second largest by total area.

'Within an hour of meeting the pastor, Rhonda had signed the necessary paperwork, and within a few weeks Anthony was officially our son. It was one of the greatest miracles I've ever been part of, and Anthony has been a deeply loved member of our family and our church community ever since.'

Speak, Lord, for your servant hears.
Grant us ears to hear,
Eyes to see,
Wills to obey,
Hearts to love.
(Christina Rossetti)

MORE ON LISTENING TO GOD:

- **PRAYER COURSE SESSION**: #7: Listening.

- **PRAYER TOOLS**: 1. How to Speak in Tongues. 2. How to do the *Lectio Divina*. 3. How to Journal. 4. How to Turn Parenting into Prayer (prayercourse.org).

- **FURTHER READING**: *Hearing God*, by Dallas Willard.

HERO OF LISTENING:

Amy Carmichael:
Wild bird child

Oh, will you pray? Stop now and pray, lest desire turn to feeling and feeling evaporate. (Amy Carmichael)

Long before anyone talked about 'human trafficking', a remarkable Irish missionary called Amy Carmichael was rescuing children from forced prostitution in India's Hindu temples.

With extraordinary resilience this single woman, who described herself as a 'wild bird child', stood up to the powerful temple priests and established two homes – for girls and boys – in the city of Dohnavur, in the Tamil Nadu State. She also started a hospital funded by the Queen of England. Amy Carmichael lived in India for fifty-five years and died there without returning to Northern Ireland.

She was also a prolific writer and poet, penning some thirty-five books. Her devotional works, which are mystical and challenging, are also startlingly honest about her own personal struggles. They often take the form of conversations with God.

As a little girl, Amy would sometimes spread out her sheets at bedtime and invite the Lord to come and sit down beside her. These intimate moments with God only seemed to deepen throughout Amy's influential life as she became increasingly acquainted with the voice of God. Her writings have inspired countless others to nurture their own daily rhythms of prayer and listening.

Amy Carmichael teaches us that listening to God does not cloister us away from reality, but rather propels us out into wild adventures, abandoned to what she referred to as 'Calvary Love'.

She was buried in Dohnavur in a grave without a head-stone, at her own request. But the children she had rescued placed a birdbath over her grave instead, inscribed with a single Tamil word: '*Amma*', which means mother.

Let us listen to simple words; our Lord speak simply:
'Trust Me, My child,' He says. 'Trust Me with a humbler heart and a fuller abandon to My will than ever thou didst before. Trust Me to pour My love through thee, as minute succeeds minute. (Amy Carmichael, *If*)[13]

10. Confession & Reconciliation

How to get right with God

'Forgive us our sins
as we forgive those who sin against us.'

To confess your sins to God is not to tell him
anything he doesn't already know. Until you confess
them, however, they are the abyss between you.
When you confess them, they become the bridge.
(Frederick Buechner)[1]

At last we come to the hardest, most challenging line of the entire Lord's Prayer. Who wouldn't want a loving Father in heaven, the kingdom of heaven to come, and a nice fresh loaf of daily bread? But then this. It sneaks up and hits us where it hurts. First the jab in the guts, 'Forgive us our sins'. No excuses. No ifs and buts. Caught red-handed. And then the right hook: 'as we forgive those who sin against us'. The only line of the Lord's Prayer that carries a big, fat caveat. If we won't forgive, we won't be forgiven. 'That's not fair!' we cry. 'He started it! She's to blame! Hey, I'm the victim here!' But clenched fists and pointing fingers close our hands to grace. 'Right here', says America's greatest living theologian, Stanley Hauerwas, 'is where the Lord's Prayer is most difficult to pray. Perhaps that's why this is the longest and most involved petition of the Lord's Prayer.'[2]

You probably remember that lovely story about a paralysed

man whose friends let him down on a stretcher through a hole in the roof. The first thing Jesus said to him was, 'Son, your sins are forgiven.' A little while later he healed his body too, but only because 'I want you to know that the Son of Man has authority on earth to forgive sins.' Interesting priorities. Wouldn't we have healed the poor man first?

IT DOESN'T MATTER WHAT YOU'VE SAID OR DONE; WHAT YOU'VE THOUGHT ABOUT SAYING OR DOING; WHERE YOU'VE BEEN OR WHO YOU'VE BEEN THERE WITH — THERE IS MORE GRACE IN GOD THAN SIN IN YOU

Our greatest need and God's greatest gift are the same thing: forgiveness of sins. And to receive it we have only to ask and pass it on. But to ask for it we must first admit that we need it. Instinctively, we wriggle. We want to pass the buck. The man blames the woman. The woman blames the snake. Anything, anyone but us. 'We make guilty of our disasters the sun, the moon, and stars,' says Shakespeare, 'as if we were villains by necessity . . . drunkards, liars, and adulterers by an enforced obedience of planetary influence.'[3]

This is the hardest line of the Lord's Prayer, but it is also by far the most outrageous. No 'please'. No 'sorry'. Just this audacious request, sounding suspiciously like a demand: 'Forgive us our sins.' In Matthew's Gospel, it is rendered, 'forgive us our *debts*', because the Greek word *opheilemata* is a commercial term, not a religious one, denoting 'something which is owed, something which is due, something which is a duty or an obligation to give or to pay. In other words, it means a debt in the widest sense of the term.'[4] The word 'forgive' has similar commercial connotations, literally meaning 'to wipe the slate clean'. Try that with your bank manager, your mortgage lender, your credit card provider: 'Dear Sir, my wife and I appear to have borrowed far more than we can afford to repay. I am writing, therefore, to ask you to erase from your hard-drive all record of everything we currently owe. Forgive us our debts. Let's call it quits. Yours faithfully, etc.' It'd be preposterous. Naive. Not the way the world works. Not the way the world works at all.

Of course, some people will splutter with indignation at all of this. They'll point out, quite rightly, that forgiveness may be simple but it isn't cheap. That it 'cost the cross'. And yet Jesus gave this prayer, and the disciples started praying it, at least a year before he died. Perhaps when they prayed 'forgive us our sins' they remembered the story of the prodigal son, stumbling stinking up the road with his fistful of mixed motives and that flimsy apology tucked in his back pocket: 'Father, I have sinned . . .' But before he could deliver it, he was hugged by the father, handed the credit card, welcomed home. It wasn't the speech. It was never the speech. It was only ever that he had come.

It doesn't matter what you've said or done; what you've thought about saying or doing; where you've been or who you've been there with – there is more grace in God than sin in you. 'He . . . always forgives', says Pope Francis; 'we get tired of asking forgiveness.'⁵ You cannot be too bad, too broken or too boring for God's unconditional love, only too proud to acknowledge how desperately you need it. Ask and you will receive. Take one step towards the Father and he'll come running towards you. Splutter that unconvincing apology and he'll hug you silent. Pray 'forgive us our sins as we forgive those who sin against us' – twelve words – and he'll do it. He'll forgive you. Just like that. He'll wipe the slate clean. Here, then, is the gospel at the heart of Christ's manifesto: if we will confess our sins to the Father, asking for his grace, we will be forgiven. Or as the Apostle John puts it elsewhere, 'If we confess our sins, he is faithful and just and will forgive us our sins and purify us from all unrighteousness.'⁶

I spent a long, sad afternoon with a friend who had cheated

on his wife. His marriage was on the rocks. His family was breaking apart. He was a Christian leader and had lost his ministry. He had confessed, but only because he had been caught. He described his predicament repeatedly as 'the perfect storm' and a 'mid-life crisis'. He explained that he had been stressed at work and unhappy in his marriage. He talked about unresolved trauma in his childhood. But in more than two hours of talking, he never once said the words he most needed to say: 'Pete, I sinned.'

When President Nixon's Special Counsel and 'hatchet man' Chuck Colson was indicted in the famous Watergate scandal that rocked America in the 1970s, his instinct was to fight. But one night he visited a friend who spoke directly into his life, accusing him of pride.

'Suddenly, I felt naked and unclean, my bravado defenses gone. I was exposed, unprotected.' As he drove away from the house, Chuck Colson finally broke down.

> With my face cupped in my hands, head leaning against the wheel, I forgot about machismo, about pretenses, about fears of being weak. And as I did, I began to experience a wonderful feeling of being released. Then came the strange sensation that water was not only running down my cheeks, but surging through my whole body as well, cleansing and cooling as it went. They weren't tears of sadness and remorse, nor of joy – but somehow, tears of relief.
>
> And then I prayed my first real prayer.[7]

* * *

Praying the *Examen*

At night I like to take a few minutes before bed to replay and review the day with the Lord using my own version of the ancient prayer of *Examen*. It's a very simple process – anyone can do it – and yet I've found it to be an extraordinarily powerful tool for confession, reconciliation and personal transformation. It's a practical way of becoming a little bit more like Jesus day by day.

There's a great deal that has been written over the last two thousand years about examining our consciences, most notably by the Jesuits who popularised the *Examen*, which advocates various steps (traditionally in Latin) for self-reflection. But because I don't understand much Latin, and generally need things to be easy if they're to be sustainable and enjoyable, I have developed my own simple four-step equivalent:

1. Replay.
2. Rejoice.
3. Repent.
4. Reboot.

1. Replay

First, replay your day in as much detail as possible. Don't just skim through its headline moments – the obvious events that featured in your calendar. Try also to recall the mundane 'in-between' interactions, the fleeting attitudes, and casual conversations that filled the cracks of your day, asking, 'Where was God when that happened?' 'Where was God in that person's behaviour?' and even, 'Where was God in that moment of pain?' One Jesuit compares this process to 'rummaging for God. Going through a drawer full of stuff, feeling around, looking for something that you are sure must be there.'[8] Rummaging is harder than you might think. In fact, I find it almost impossible to recall the details of most days unless I work through them chronologically. But as you do this, you will quickly discover that the devil is in the detail, but so too are the angels. On an average day there's much for which to repent, but even more for which to rejoice. There are 550 references to remembering in the Bible. It is by remembering that we start to see how present God is in our lives – at work in all things, all people, all places, and at all times.

2. Rejoice

As you rummage through the drawer of your day, you will discover currency, forgotten jewellery, precious photographs, dull nuggets of gold. Night after night you will marvel at the furtive ways God has blessed you, the frequency of his whispers, the consistency of his presence, the lightness of his touch. Perhaps you will recall the joy of bumping into a friend unexpectedly in the street; the ridiculous video that made you laugh, the unexpected hug from your teenage son, the cup of fresh coffee in an earthenware mug, the lyric that moved you, the drumming of rain against the window while you worked indoors in your socks, the cloud formations and the rays of light that followed the storm, and now the quietness of this night, the stars above, and the exquisite prospect of your own warm bed.

But God is not just in the nice stuff. He is also with us 'in the darkest valley' (Ps. 23:4), in our seasons of doubt (John 20:27), and even in our sin (John 8:7). In my own life, I may not be able to see *why* God hasn't healed Sammy's chronic illness (and I don't think he's about to tell me), but I can certainly see *where* he is at work within it and through it. Generally I find it more useful, therefore, to pray 'where?' rather than 'why?' prayers. 'Where were you, Lord, in our medical appointment today?' 'Where are you now in our weariness and disappointment?' David G. Benner puts it like this: 'Unwelcome circumstances are not gifts. But they may contain a gift.'[9] The prayer of *Examen* enables us to receive and unwrap those gifts.

3. Repent

As you replay your day in detail, rejoicing in the evidence of God's blessings, you will also, inevitably, be reminded of actions, words, thoughts and attitudes that were wrong. In the stillness of prayer, the Holy Spirit will often highlight occasions when you were selfish, lustful, deceitful, pompous, hurtful and unkind. Things that may have been relatively easy to justify or ignore in the swirl of the moment, become so much harder to excuse under the direct gaze of God. Whenever our dirty little secrets, which flourish like fungi in the darkness, are exposed to the surgical brilliance of his light, we can try to conceal them, like Adam and Eve 'who hid from the LORD God among the trees of the garden',[10] or we can pretend they're not there, like the Pharisee praying, 'God, I thank you that I am not like other people', or we can hold up our hands and confess them like the tax collector crying out, 'God, have mercy on me, a sinner.' Truly, says Jesus, 'this man, rather than the other, went home justified before God'.[11]

You probably take a regular bath or shower to remove the dirt from your body. In just the same way you are invited to come to God regularly, praying, 'Cleanse me . . . and I shall be clean; wash me, and I shall be whiter than snow' (Ps. 51:7). Without this discipline, you will begin to stink! Behaviours that would once have seemed shameful or even shocking will become tolerated, accommodated and eventually normalised as your conscience is numbed. But by confessing your sins regularly, your life will smell sweet! You will be healthy and holy – a little bit more like Jesus each day.

4. Reboot

Having replayed the day in detail, rejoicing and repenting along the way, we turn our attention to the challenges of tomorrow, asking for God's strength to live a little more for his glory. The Apostle Paul says that we are 'transformed into his image with ever-increasing glory',[12] but how does this actually take place? Is it just a mystery? An automatic thing that happens regardless of the choices we make? Sadly we've all met enough cantankerous old Christians to realise that there's nothing inevitable about sanctification. I believe that it is received incrementally day by day, choice by choice, as we train our brains to 'rejoice always' and incline our hearts again and again away from the shadows and towards the light.

* * *

I was walking the darkened streets near our house one night, reviewing the day in this way as usual before bed, remembering how I'd driven Sammy and the boys to the cinema, and how someone had cut us up. I'd yelled at him. Sammy had yelled at me. I'd yelled at Sammy. Hadn't she seen how dangerously the other guy was driving? Had she forgotten that we had vulnerable children in the car? Didn't she know there was such a thing as righteous anger? She'd gone silent. We'd arrived at the cinema. The film had been great. Life had moved on. No big deal.

But now in the stillness of these darkened streets as I returned to that moment it seemed that God was siding with my wife. I sighed. 'OK, I'm sorry. I admit it: I lost my temper. I shouldn't have yelled at that driver. Lord, help me to be more patient tomorrow.'

There was a pause before I sensed him telling me to apologise to our sons. This thought annoyed me and I found myself protesting. 'That's ridiculous. You're making this bigger than it is. My kids don't need me to apologise. They won't even remember such a trivial incident. Do you have any idea what the traffic is like round here?'

Ten minutes later I was sitting on Hudson's bed. 'Son, I just want to say sorry to you for something. Do you remember me yelling at that man on the way to the cinema?' Immediately he nodded. 'I shouldn't have done that. Mum was right. Christians are supposed to be patient and kind. I set you a bad example. That's not how I want you to grow up and treat people. I'm sorry.' Immediately he put his arms around my neck and squeezed me tight. 'That's OK Dad.'

A minute later I was in the room next door, making the same speech to Danny, and the same thing happened. He immediately knew exactly what I was talking about. He hadn't forgotten either. He listened to my apology and didn't think it was crazy. He hugged me and told me it was OK.

It's a silly, mundane story, and that's the whole point. We are changed – conformed into the likeness of Christ – through a thousand small choices like these.

Millions of people have found freedom from addictions through the Twelve Step Programme, the fifth step of which is simple confession: 'We admit to God, to ourselves and to another human being the exact nature of our wrongs.' There is such power in confessing our sins, not just to God but to another person. Again and again I have found relief and release in the simple act of admitting my failures, bringing them into the light. God sent me back into the house that night to confess to my sons, and in their hugs I received absolution. 'Confess your sins *to each other*', not just to God, 'and pray for each other so that you may be healed', says the Apostle James (James 5:16). Elsewhere Jesus says, 'If you are offering your gift at the altar and there remember that your brother or sister has something against you, leave your gift there in front of the altar. First go and be reconciled to them; then come and offer your gift.'[13]

Where else does the Bible command us to worship God second?

The anarchic comedian Russell Brand, formerly renowned for his debauched life of drug and sex addiction, has written a surprising paean to the Twelve Step Programme through which, he says, he has found freedom and hope. 'Confession returned me to the wholeness of myself and the wholeness of the world,' he says. 'It was restorative.'[14] We cannot detach our relationships with people from our relationship with God. We cannot be more reconciled with him than we are with our neighbour.[15] Our prayer lives and our family lives are intricately interwoven. It is 'as we forgive those who sin against us' that we ourselves receive forgiveness from God.

Reconciliation

At the age of six, Ruby Bridges was volunteered by her mother to become the first African American girl to attend an all-white elementary school in Louisiana, New Orleans. Each day she had to be escorted to and from the school by up to twenty-five

Federal Marshals to protect her from the crowd of angry protesters at the school gates. One woman would regularly scream death threats at Ruby. Another protester held a black doll aloft in a coffin. Every parent pulled their child out of the school.

Having braved the crowd's hatred, Ruby would sit all alone in an empty classroom. She was taught by Barbara Henry, the only teacher willing to offer her an education. In her breaks she recalls wandering the school, looking for all the other children. Images of this tiny little girl – so smartly dressed and clutching her school bag, guarded by suited men twice her size – polarised America. Norman Rockwell depicted the scene in a famous painting, *The Problem We All Live With*.

Watching this tragedy unfold, child psychologist Robert Coles offered Ruby counselling. Once a week he sat in the humble home she shared with four siblings and her parents, who could neither read nor write.

'You looked like you were talking to the people in the street on your way into school yesterday,' he said on one occasion. 'Did you finally get angry with them? Were you telling them to leave you alone?'

'No, doctor,' replied Ruby politely. 'I didn't tell them anything. I didn't talk to them.'

'Well, who were you talking to?'

The little girl stared at him. 'I was talking to God. I was praying to God for the people in the street.'

'You were *praying* for them? But Ruby, why were you praying for them?'

Her eyes widened. 'Well, don't you think they need praying for?'

Robert Coles was lost for words. Regaining his composure he whispered, 'What do you say when you pray for them, Ruby?'

'Oh, I always say the same thing. Please God, try to forgive these people because even if they say these mean things, they don't know what they're doing.'[16]

* * *

On 8 November 1987 a forty-pound bomb planted by the Provisional IRA exploded in the small, Northern Irish town of Enniskillen, killing eleven innocent people and injuring sixty-four. One of those killed was Marie Wilson, a local nurse whose last words, spoken to her father Gordon Wilson buried in the rubble beside her, were, 'Daddy, I love you very much.'

Gordon Wilson was pulled from the rubble alive and, in an astonishing interview recorded just hours after the bombing, still in shock amid the agony of losing his daughter, he told the BBC, 'I bear no ill will. I bear no grudge. Dirty sort of talk is not going to bring her back to life. She was a great wee lassie. She loved her profession. She was a pet. She's dead. She's in heaven and we shall meet again. I will pray for these men tonight and every night.' That interview echoed to the far corners of the world. Wilson's pleas for peace and his example of forgiveness prevented reprisals and shook the IRA to its core. In fact, on the tenth anniversary of the Enniskillen atrocity, its political wing Sinn Féin issued an unprecedented formal apology. Gordon Wilson, a humble provincial draper, had changed the course of history by choosing to forgive his enemies. One hardened journalist reviewing his own career said that interviewing Gordon Wilson had been 'the nearest I'd ever get to being in the presence of a saint'.

Jesus calls us to forgive those who sin against us. This is how the cycles of hatred can be broken. It's what he models for us on the cross, praying, 'Father, forgive them, for they do not know what they are doing.'[17] It's what six-year-old Ruby Bridges modelled in New Orleans, praying, 'Please God, forgive these people . . . they don't know what they're doing.' It's what Gordon Wilson modelled in Northern Ireland saying, 'I bear no grudge . . . I will pray for these men tonight and every night.' Prayer was the instinctive response of each one.

The Lord's Prayer is a cry for reconciliation at every level

– in our broken relationship with God ('Our Father in heaven, hallowed be your name'), in our broken relationships with one another ('forgive us as we forgive'), and in our broken relationship with the world ('let your kingdom come on earth'). In fact, this line about forgiving those who sin against us can be applied to every other line of the prayer. Our Father's name is hallowed as we forgive. His kingdom comes as we forgive. We are forgiven as we forgive.

Our world is bitterly divided between left and right, black and white, rich and poor, East and West, liberal and conservative, women and men, religious fundamentalism and free-market capitalism. The lawyer and apologist Michael Ramsden says that the three most powerful words in the English language are currently: 'I am offended.'[18] Families are breaking apart. Societies are fragmenting. International alliances are ending. Politics is polarising. Tribalism, nationalism and protectionism are proliferating. At such a time, we simply cannot separate our prayers for the coming of God's kingdom from Christ's radical call to be reconciled with those who sin against us. Reconciliation is what the coming of his kingdom looks like! Jesus says: 'Love your enemies and pray for those who persecute you.'[19] The Apostle Paul says that 'God, who reconciled us to himself through Christ' has given us 'the ministry of reconciliation'.[20]

Ruby Bridges and Gordon Wilson ministered reconciliation in situations that were socially extreme and their examples are undeniably extraordinary, but we can all follow them in less dramatic ways. Whenever we're offended and hurt, we can choose to forgive. We can remain silent on social media when our views are attacked. We can deny ourselves the sugary sympathy of victimhood. We can love and pray for those who would otherwise be our enemies. Jesus says that as we do so – as we stop pointing fingers, unclench our fists, and open our palms – the Father will give us grace.

There are probably people in your life who have hurt you deeply, and the idea of forgiving them may well be very painful, but until you choose to forgive, they will still have a hold on your heart. Unforgiveness, it is said, is like drinking poison and waiting for the other person to die. Forgiving is not naive. It isn't forgetting. It's not saying that what the other person said or did was OK in any way. It doesn't mean leaving yourself exposed to future attack. Forgiving may involve talking to a friend, getting counselling, or even going to the police. But forgiveness is the choice to love and let go, not to hate and hold on. It tends to be a process, as we choose to forgive again and again, or as Jesus puts it, 'not seven times, but seventy-seven times'.[21]

On 27 June 1995, Gordon Wilson was finally reunited with his daughter Marie. No one really knows how many lives he saved, the spiral of bloodshed he prevented, the soul-searching he provoked, by forgiving her killers. But when he gave that raw BBC interview just hours after the tragedy, the world could hear that Gordon Wilson's reactions were sincere; not politically calculated but spiritually inculcated. Here was a heartbroken dad and a simple follower of Jesus who had trained himself in the secrecy of his own prayer life over years to love and forgive those who hurt him, never knowing how deeply his resolve would be tested, nor how powerfully it would be used. Looking back on the legacy of this humble Irish draper's heroic act of forgiveness, the historian Jonathan Bardon makes an extraordinary assertion: 'No words in more than twenty-five years of violence in Northern Ireland had such a powerful, emotional impact.'[22]

On 15 July 2011, Ruby Bridges was invited by President Barack Obama to the White House, where Norman Rockwell's painting of her walking to school in front of graffiti saying 'Nigger' was temporarily on display. The two of them stood there looking at it, reading that word, the first African American girl to attend Louisiana's William Frantz Elementary School, and the first African American Commander in Chief. He turned to Ruby eventually and said, 'If it hadn't been for you guys, I might not be here and we wouldn't be looking at this together.' How had

this happened? Ruby had been courageous and dignified and
remarkable but she had also been just six years old. She had
inculcated grace quietly at home, been taught to pray for her
persecutors by her poor, illiterate parents.

Ruby Bridges and Gordon Wilson remind us that our choices
to forgive can change the world, breaking cycles of bitterness,
healing divisions and multiplying the fractals of grace. Without
forgiveness all our prayers – all the things described elsewhere
in this book – are dead religion. But when we forgive those
who hurt us, the Father's name is hallowed, his kingdom comes
and we ourselves are forgiven.

*   *   *

In this chapter we have covered a lot of ground. We looked at
the power of confessing our sins 'vertically' to God through the
prayer of *Examen*, and 'horizontally' to others through mutual
accountability and the extraordinary way in which such choices
to forgive can help to reconcile a broken world.

When King David raped Bathsheba (for that is surely what
it was), and had her husband killed, God sent the prophet
Nathan to expose the magnitude of his sin. David's behaviour
had been monstrous, but his response has become perhaps the
greatest prayer of repentance of all time:

> Have mercy on me, O God, according to your unfailing
>   love;
> according to your great compassion blot out my
>   transgressions.
> Wash away all my iniquity and cleanse me from my sin.
> For I know my transgressions, and my sin is always
>   before me . . .
> Create in me a pure heart, O God, and renew a steadfast
>   spirit within me.
> (Ps. 51:1–3, 10)

MORE ON CONFESSION & RECONCILATION:

- **PRAYER COURSE SESSION**: This is an 'extra' chapter without an equivalent in The Prayer Course. Week off!

- **PRAYER TOOLS**: 1. How to Pray the Jesus Prayer. 2. How to Confess. 3. Identificational Repentance (prayercourse.org).

- **FURTHER READING**: *The Lost Art of Forgiving*, by Johann Christoph Arnold.

HERO OF CONFESSION & RECONCILIATION:

Archbishop Desmond Tutu:
Rabble-rouser for peace

Without forgiveness there is no future. (Desmond Tutu)

'I am sorry' are three of the hardest words we will ever say, laughs the retired Archbishop of Johannesburg and Cape Town. Desmond Tutu is now a global statesman, having been awarded the Nobel Peace Prize for his central role in the campaign to dismantle apartheid.

At the invitation of his friend Nelson Mandela, Tutu famously established the Truth and Reconciliation Commission, which granted perpetrators of violence the opportunity to confess to those they had wronged, and appeal for forgiveness. The violence in South Africa under apartheid had been so widespread and so systemic that incarceration of every offender would have been both impossible and self-destructive. Tutu's conviction, therefore, rooted in the teachings of Jesus, was that confession could help victims to find healing, and perpetrators to receive forgiveness. The results stunned the world as Tutu took the principles of confession out of private pietism and into the heart of the public square, engendering a type of social holiness that began to pervade the nation and reduce violence.

A few years ago, I had the privilege of interviewing 'Arch', as he is commonly addressed, and asked him how he had sustained the fire in his belly through so many years. Without hesitation he replied, 'Oh, through prayer. It is prayer that puts fuel on the fire.' Sure enough, in a corner of his small backyard in Orlando West stands a brightly coloured prayer room, which he has visited several times a day, ever since 1993 when a nun challenged him about the priority of prayer. At that time South Africa was teetering on the precipice of civil war. 'You have been a celebrity too long,' chided the nun, 'and it is taking a toll, not only on you but also on those around you. You need once more to realise your nothingness before God.'

Desmond Tutu could so easily have been consumed with bitterness, not peace. Growing up as a black man under apartheid with an alcoholic and violent father, he could have responded with violence, but chose to forgive. 'My father has long since died,' he told the *Guardian* newspaper in 2014, 'but if I could speak to him today, I would want to tell him that I had forgiven him.'

11: Spiritual Warfare

How to exercise spiritual authority

'Lead us not into temptation,
Deliver us from the evil one.'

———————

Enemy-occupied territory, that is what this world is.
Christianity is the story of how the rightful king has landed,
you might say landed in disguise, and is calling us
to take part in a great campaign of sabotage.
(C.S. Lewis – *Mere Christianity*)[1]

Raymond Edman was dying of typhus fever at the age of twenty-five in the jungles of Ecuador. His doctor – a specialist in tropical diseases – had advised Raymond's wife to start preparing his funeral. Men were already making his coffin. Edith was busy dyeing her wedding dress black.

But that same day, three thousand miles north of Ecuador, in Attleboro, Massachusetts, Raymond's uncle Joe became deeply, inexplicably troubled. He knew nothing of his nephew's actual predicament, but couldn't shake the sense that he was in some kind of grave danger. Joe, who was attending a conference at the time, felt so stirred that he persuaded its two hundred delegates to join him in urgent intercession for Raymond to be 'delivered from evil', even though none of them knew the nature of the evil they were to fight. The conference rose up and prayed so fervently that, years later, many of those present still recalled the intensity. Consumed with a sense of imminent danger they fasted lunch and continued interceding until the middle of the afternoon, at which point a great peace settled upon them. The sense of danger subsided. Somehow they knew that their prayers had been heard – that Raymond Edman, far away in Ecuador, had been delivered from evil.

Meanwhile Raymond had fallen unconscious and, in his comatose state, became aware of a loving presence slowly entering the room, rising from the ground to the level of his bed and eventually filling the building. 'I experienced a sweet sense of the love of God in Christ, such as I had never known before in all the years of my life,' he recalled. 'It is sufficient to say that I have no fear of dying.'[2] He felt himself ascending with great joy, until a quiet voice told him to return. To the amazement of those preparing his funeral, Raymond Edman regained consciousness and was completely healed. In later life he would become President of Wheaton College and a mentor to the great evangelist Billy Graham. 'We will never know the full evaluation of his life and ministry until we stand at the judgement seat of Christ,' said Billy, 'but still I have to say that he was the most unforgettable Christian I ever met.'[3]

Deliver us from evil

Raymond Edman's life was a testament to the urgency and power of a particular kind of prayer. His uncle Joe, and those at the conference in Massachusetts, engaged in a form of author-itative and fervent intercession against specific enemy attack. On that day they waged war in 'the heavenly realms'[4] and won. Raymond Edman was delivered from evil. Their prayers thwarted a life-threatening disease and saved his life.

The Bible is quite clear that we are at war. There is a vicious battle raging all around us between the kingdom of God and the tyranny of a cruel insurgency. 'There is no neutral ground in the universe,' says C.S. Lewis. 'Every square inch, every split second, is claimed and counter claimed by Satan.'[5] This name 'Satan' literally just means 'the enemy' or 'the adversary'. Jesus describes him as 'the thief [who] comes to steal and kill and destroy'.[6] When a twenty-five-year-old missionary in Ecuador is about to die of a tropical disease and his uncle has to be supernaturally alerted to pray for his protection, we can be fairly sure that the thief has come to steal and kill and destroy. But Jesus continues, 'I have come that they may have life, and have it to the full.' And so, through the earnest prayers of that conference in Massachusetts, Satan's strategy to terminate a beautiful life before it could bear its full fruit was resoundingly defeated. Death was countered by life.

Since 'there is no neutral ground in the universe', as C.S. Lewis says, there can be no neutral people. Every one of us must pick a side. No one gets to be a conscientious objector. We are all called, in the words of the musician Bruce Cockburn, to 'kick at the darkness 'til it bleeds daylight'.[7]

Put your fists together and pray
We must all practise violence and remember that he who prays is fighting against the devil and the flesh. Satan is opposed to the church . . . the best thing we can do, therefore, is to put our fists together and pray. (Martin Luther)[8]

Spiritual warfare tends not to be meek and mild, but forceful, assertive and authoritative. It is sometimes accompanied by fasting and generally requires perseverance and careful spiritual discernment.[9] There are three things you really need to know to be effective in this kind of prayer:

1. You must know your enemy.
2. You must know your authority.
3. You must know how to fight.

1. Know your enemy
Be alert and of sober mind. Your enemy the devil prowls around like a roaring lion looking for someone to devour. (1 Pet. 5:8)

I'm aware that talk of Satan, demons, fallen angels, and an apocalyptic battle between cosmic forces of light and darkness, will sound ridiculous to some, and like a plot from a second-rate Marvel comic to others. In the West we have, for the most part, replaced biblical cosmology with humanistic psychology, sociology and anthropology. Every sin is attributed to a societal or clinical cause. And yet – for all our supposed sophistication – we remain acutely aware of evil at work in our world. Our news cycles report acts of unspeakable horror almost every day. People who rape children, imprison strangers, torture animals, or drop sarin bombs on civilians, are invariably branded 'evil'. And away from the spotlight of public disdain, we remain acutely aware within ourselves of dark shadows lurking – our own shocking capacity to hate, to hurt, to use and abuse others.

There's a fascinating encounter near the start of the horror film *The Silence of the Lambs* in which Clarice Starling, a young FBI trainee, asks the cannibalistic serial killer Hannibal Lecter what happened to make him so twisted. 'Nothing happened to me, Officer Starling,' he purrs. 'I happened. You can't reduce me to a set of influences. You've given up good and evil for behaviourism, Officer Starling. You've got everyone in moral dignity pants. Nothing is ever anyone's fault. Look at me. Can you stand to say I'm evil?'

'Modern people cannot answer the monster's question,' concedes the liberal intellectual Andrew Delbanco in his book, *The Death of Satan: How Americans Have Lost the Sense of Evil*. 'A gulf has opened up in our culture', he writes, 'between the visibility of evil and the intellectual resources to cope with it . . .'

> We have jettisoned in the West the idea of cosmic evil, or transcendent evil, or supernatural evil. We don't believe in it. In fact, we don't like to use the word evil because it implies moral absolutes and value judgements. So we use medical terms. We talk about dysfunction. We talk about pathology. We don't use moral terminology. But as the twentieth century has gone on it has gotten harder and harder to say that holocausts and ethnic cleansing and serial killing is just bad psychological and sociological adjustment.[10]

Near the end of the Second World War, a pastor called Helmut Thielicke preached a poignant sermon in the German city of Stuttgart, applying this last line of the Lord's Prayer – 'deliver us from evil' – to the atrocities of Nazism and the decimation of the European continent during the years of conflict:

> Dear friends, in our time we have had far too much contact with demonic powers;
>   we have sensed and seen how men and whole movements have been corrupted and controlled by mysterious, abysmal powers, leading them where they had no intention of going;
>   year by year we have seen an increasingly poisonous atmosphere settling down upon our globe and we sense how real and almost tangible are the evil spirits in the air, seeing an invisible hand passing an invisible cup of poison from nation to nation and throwing them into confusion.[11]

From Helmut Thielicke to Hannibal Lecter, the biblical cosmology of good versus evil makes sense of our broken world. It stands the test of time because it rings true with our universal human experience. 'Humankind is losing faith in the liberal story that dominated politics in recent decades', admits the liberal historian Yuval Noah Harari in his best-selling *21 Lessons for the 21st Century*.[12] Secularism is partly losing credibility because of the way it attempts to deconstruct ancient moral absolutes without offering any satisfactory alternative explanation for the reality of evil in our world. So let's go back to the ancient texts and see what the Gospels say . . .

Jesus versus Satan
When we read the text objectively, the Jesus of the Gospels begins to look like the kind of apocalyptic mystic who would not fit at all well in the lecture halls of most seminaries, let alone behind the lectern on an average Sunday morning. Here is a man who launched his public ministry with more than a month of intensive spiritual warfare, locked in hand-to-hand

combat with Satan in the wilderness.[13] On one occasion he claimed to have seen 'Satan fall like lightning from heaven'.[14] He concluded his Lord's Prayer with a disconcerting cry for help and the alarming word 'evil', which isn't the way you're supposed to conclude great creedal prayers. The early church took it upon themselves to add a doxology ('for the kingdom, the glory and the power are yours . . .'), partly, I suspect, just to round things off on a less alarming note. Throughout his short public ministry, Jesus encountered demons and regularly set people free from their control. He performed miracles and taught a great deal more about spiritual warfare than most pastors do today.[15] And then, at the Last Supper, Jesus warned Peter that 'Satan has asked to sift all of you as wheat' (we can only guess how he knew). 'But I have prayed for you . . . that your faith may not fail.'[16]

My eyes were first opened to the reality of spiritual warfare when I lived and worked among the poor in Hong Kong. It was wonderful to witness men finding freedom from heroin addiction and Triad gangs, but when the dragon boat races and other Buddhist festivals took place we seemed to experience intense spiritual attack. More of the 'brothers' would run away and relapse. Sometimes those who had been doing well would suddenly become violent. Occasionally there were suicides. It was so predictable that we would rota extra staff in advance and increase our prayer cover pre-emptively. I learned to look at the smiling Buddhas in their ornate shrines with their offerings of incense sticks and plates of oranges, and see that behind the cheap plastic ornaments lurked dark spiritual powers. It all seemed so clear to me in that context.

When eventually I returned to the leafy Home Counties of England I wondered where all the demons had gone! The powers that had been so obvious in Hong Kong seemed completely absent, or at least invisible, in my own culture. But as I prayed I began to see that the way we fetishise the shopping mall, the hours we spend worshipping at the shrine of social media, even the way some men spend their Sunday mornings kneeling before their cars, is really not so different to the way those rural Chinese offer oranges and incense to plastic Buddhas in Hong Kong. As the scholar N.T. Wright says: 'When human beings worship that which is not God, they give authority to forces of destruction and malevolence; and those forces gain a power.'[17]

Against the powers
Our struggle is not against flesh and blood, but against the rulers, against the authorities, against the powers of this dark world and against the spiritual forces of evil in the heavenly realms. (Eph. 6:12)

All human institutions and organisations, from golf clubs to governments, eventually develop a culture that is greater than the sum of their parts; more powerful than any of the individuals involved. These cultures can be positive or negative. For instance, companies like Motown Records in the 1960s, or Apple Inc. in the first decade of this century, became hothouses of extraordinary innovation. Law-enforcement agencies can become institutionally racist or sexist (and significantly this is not easily changed, even when a member of the oppressed group is put in charge). There are all sorts of sociological and anthropological explanations for this effect, but the Bible teaches that there are also spiritual realities at play.[18]

While living in exile under the Babylonian regime, the great biblical hero Daniel received a disturbing revelation from God one day about a great impending war. Understanding his authority and the power of prayer, Daniel began to intercede, fasting meat, alcohol and even 'body lotion'. When we are facing a significant battle, and needing a particular breakthrough, it's always worth considering some form of bodily self-denial. Fasting can help to focus our prayers the way a magnifying glass focuses sunlight to start a fire. This might mean going without food, sex, social media or even, in Daniel's case, soap! (See Tool-shed: *How to Fast.*)

After three weeks of fasting and prayer, an angel appeared to Daniel with an extraordinary message: 'Since the first day that you set your mind to gain understanding and to humble yourself before your God, your words were heard, and I have come in response to them. But the prince of the Persian kingdom resisted me twenty-one days.'[19] And then the angel says: 'Soon I will return to fight against the prince of Persia, and when I go, the prince of Greece will come . . . No one supports me against them except Michael, your prince.'

This encounter provides a fascinating insight into the spiritual battle that goes on in the heavenly realm when we pray, and also into the time lapse that may require our perseverance in prayer. It also hints that there are particular angelic powers ('princes') over different geographical regions and cultural entities (principalities).

Some people have read too much into this passage. They map the entire world with hierarchies of 'tutelary spirits' presiding over every nation and guardian angels allocated to every saint. It's way beyond the remit of this 'simple guide for normal people' to get into such esoteric discussions, so let me just make two uncontroversial observations. First, the Bible does indeed teach that there are spiritual powers at work in our world, affecting organisations and cultures as well as individuals. Second, as citizens of heaven we must exercise great discernment so that we can stand against these powers. 'What you are up against, in being saved', says the eminent theologian Stanley Hauerwas, 'is not simply your personal faults and foibles, your petty temptations and peccadilloes:

> You are up against what we call 'the principalities and powers'.
> Evil is large, cosmic, organized, subtle, pervasive, and real. The
> powers never appear as evil or coercive. The powers always
> masquerade as freedoms that we have been graciously given
> or as necessities that we cannot live without.[20]

2. Know your authority
Many Christians have no problem at all recognising the reality of principalities and powers at work in our world (especially

if they come from cultures that bypassed the Enlightenment), but they do not necessarily understand their own personal authority to contend against such dark forces and win.

Our children used to have a pet hamster called Snuffles with an uncanny knack of escaping her cage. Snuffles was the Houdini of hamsters. We also have a large, much-loved Labradoodle called Noodle, who has never knowingly been unkind to another living thing. She is the kindest, gentlest, most submissive and compliant dog you could ever meet.

On one occasion when Snuffles had once again made a valiant break for freedom, she finally met Noodle. Finding herself staring up at this vast mountain of wolf, Snuffles froze. The two animals eyeballed each other for a while and then we watched in amazement as Noodle began to cower. She laid down and rolled onto her back. The dog, we realised, was actually trying to submit to the hamster.

I think we can agree that it's ridiculous for a 65-pound carnivore to fear a tiny dumb rodent that eats its own poop. Confronted by a mere mouthful of fluff, Noodle said in effect, 'Please don't hurt me. Please like me. You can be the boss.'

Too many people are timid in their prayers and terrified in their dealings with the Enemy. The moment they behold him they roll over and submit because they don't understand who they are in Christ, how highly favoured and powerful they actually are.

IN PRAYER WE ARE LEARING TO RULE AND REIGN WITH CHRIST

The Apostle Paul addresses this very problem in his letter to the Ephesians. The city of Ephesus was riddled with idolatry, weird sexual practices and the occult. Vulnerable young Christians needed to know that Jesus was Lord and to understand the authority they had in him.

God raised him from death and set him on a throne in deep heaven, in charge of running the universe, everything from galaxies to governments, no name and no power exempt from his rule. And not just for the time being, but *forever*. He is in charge of it all. (Eph. 1:20–21, MSG)

Having cast this awesome vision of Jesus high and lifted up, 'in charge of it all', Paul tells the Ephesians something utterly astounding. He says that those of us who are 'in Christ' – a term he uses 164 times instead of 'Christian'[21] – are right up there in heaven with him since, 'God raised us up with Christ and seated us with him in the heavenly realms' (2:6).

We have been 'raised up with Christ'. Isn't that mind-blowing? It means that, when we pray, we don't just plead for mercy from the midst of the mess, but rather we exercise authority from above, as those seated with Christ 'in heavenly places'. We don't have to roll over helplessly and submit to Satan's schemes, like Noodle before the hamster, because we are sons and daughters of the King, commissioned to rule and reign by his side. This elevated perspective changes everything about how we view ourselves, how we view the world's problems, how we view God, and how we view prayer. In prayer we are learning to rule and reign with Christ.[22] When we intercede we are discovering how to implement God's government in a particular place on earth. When we engage in spiritual warfare, we don the mantle we have been given as sons and daughters of the King. It's ridiculous when you just roll over and submit to the Enemy. It's time to rise up and take authority over your life because you are 'in Christ' and 'God [has] placed all things under his feet' (Eph. 1:22).

You may well be thinking by now, 'OK fine, but if I am seated in heavenly places with Christ; if I am really being trained to rule and reign with him; if I have actually been entrusted with such incredible authority, why don't I see more miracles? Why is there still so much suffering? Why does the Enemy still seem so much more powerful than me?'

A tale of two kingdoms

On 23 June 2018 twelve members of a junior football team in northern Thailand decided to explore the Tham Luang Nang Non cave with their twenty-five-year-old coach. They were deep underground when a monsoon flooded the cave entrance. Terrified, they huddled in complete darkness almost three miles inside the cave, wondering whether they would ever feel sunlight on their skin again.

Their plight hit the news cycles around the world. More than nine hundred police officers, one hundred divers and two thousand soldiers gathered with the world's media at the mouth of the cave, but for nine days no one could find the boys. The world watched on tenterhooks, fearing the worst but hoping for the best, as a billion gallons of water were pumped out of the cave.

On 2 July a diving team managed to get deep into the cave's network of tunnels, crawling, climbing and swimming against the current with zero visibility. After more than six hours, against diminishing odds, they discovered the boys alive, huddled together high on a shelf in a cavern called 'The Hidden City'. Cold, scared and starving, they had no idea how long they'd been lost, nor how many people were looking and praying for them, but they were saved!

The watching world breathed a sigh of relief. Everyone anticipated an imminent happy ending on the following day's news. How difficult could it be to get twelve kids out of a cave? But their ordeal was far from over. Getting the boys out was going to be an arduous, dangerous process with tragic consequences, and it would take another eight days.

For those watching and praying, the wait seemed like an age. For those inside it must have been an eternity. And then, on the fourteenth day, five days after they'd been found and one day before the evacuation plan was due to be triggered, one of the divers, a former Thai Navy SEAL named Saman Kunan, drowned while delivering oxygen tanks to the boys. If a professional diver had died, how could untrained, malnourished children ever hope to escape alive?

The very next day the first of the boys was sedated, given oxygen, and slowly brought out of the cave. It was a five-hour journey, much of it under water, a gruelling process that had to be meticulously repeated for each boy over a three-day period. Having been lost since 23 June, and found since 2 July, the last boys were only finally rescued on 10 July, more than two weeks after entering the cave.

The Bible teaches, and our own experience testifies, that we live in the dark days of hope between 2 and 10 July. We've been found, but not yet fully rescued. Our salvation process has undoubtedly begun and we have great hope, but our captivity, our days of darkness, are far from over.

Unable to free ourselves we had no idea that all heaven's resources had been sent forth on a search-and-rescue mission for us. We had little choice but to wait in the dark caverns of despair, helplessly hoping and praying, like the members of that Thai football team, for salvation.

But then the miracle happened, our prayers were answered. Somehow we were found. A little light entered our darkness. It was all we needed to see. Hope overwhelmed us. Love reached us from another world. We knew that we were saved!

It's hard to imagine what that football team went through as they waited a further eight days to be freed – except that it speaks to our own state of constraint and hope. There must have been times of great joy and excitement as they anticipated their favourite food, their parents' hugs, a warm bed. But they must also have experienced great frustration in the waiting, deep distress for the man who'd died saving them, and sheer terror at the thought of the ordeal to come.

When Jesus cried out from the cross 'It is finished!' he was declaring the death of death, the cure for suffering, the remission of sin. In that single moment we were found. Light entered the caverns of our captivity. Hope dispelled despair. We were saved by the sacrifice of another. And yet here we are still waiting, still suffering, still anticipating the freedom to come. And so, although we know that we have been saved, we 'groan inwardly as we wait eagerly' (Rom. 8:23) for the full freedom for which Christ has set us free (Gal. 5:1). We have been handed a torch and it is the most precious thing in the world to us, yet we yearn with all our might for the true light of the sun, and the stars in the sky. Yes we've been rescued but we must still keep praying 'deliver us from evil'.

The theologian Tom Wright says that 'To pray "deliver us from evil" is to inhale the victory of the cross, and thereby to hold the line for another moment, another hour, another day, against the forces of destruction within ourselves and the world.'[23] We don't know how many more hours or days we must 'hold the line' within the dark caverns of this life, but we have every reason to hope. Christ's cross means that we have been found, and his resurrection assures us that we shall one day soon be free!

Finishing the job

Satan may be a vanquished foe whose demise is inevitable, but the aggression of his death-throes remains terrifying. 'He is filled with fury, because he knows that his time is short' (Rev. 12:12). We have all cried out for loved ones to be healed but, unlike Raymond Edman, they have died. We have prayed for friends to find freedom in Jesus but, unlike those boys in the cave, they remain in captivity. We have prayed and prayed against injustices, to no apparent avail. There is not always a happy ending and it is agony to lose such battles, but we are assured that the ultimate victory has been won. The biblical scholar Chuck Lowe puts it graphically:

> Like a wounded and cornered animal, Satan thrashes around desperately with the aim of injuring as many of his enemy as possible, before his own destruction . . . So the defeat of Satan does not mean the end of trouble for the church. To the contrary, it signals an escalation and intensification of opposition and persecution. But the end is in sight, and those who endure to the end shall be victorious even if, in the meantime, they become victims.[24]

3. Know how to fight

To engage in effective spiritual warfare you need to know your enemy and your authority, but most of all you need to know how to fight! The Baptist pastor John Piper says that, 'the number one reason why prayer malfunctions in the hands of believers is that we try to turn a wartime walkie-talkie into a domestic intercom. Until you know that life is war, you cannot know what prayer is for.'[25]

There are three questions you should always ask when confronting any kind of conflict in prayer:

1. *Diagnosis*: What is the Enemy's strategy against this person or place? To answer this question you will need common sense (it's often quite obvious), wisdom (not all bad things that happen are necessarily demonic), and spiritual discernment (Satan can be a convincing liar). In 1 Corinthians 12, the Apostle Paul includes the ability of 'distinguishing between spirits' in his list of all the great spiritual gifts alongside things like prophecy and healing. We need to ask the Lord, therefore, to open our eyes to see and to understand what's going on in the spiritual realm all around us, just as Elisha prayed for his terrified servant '"Open his eyes, Lord, so that he may see." Then the Lord opened the servant's eyes, and he looked and saw the hills full of horses and chariots of fire all around.'[26]

2. *Prognosis*: Having diagnosed the problem, ask yourself, 'What might God's better plan be for this person or place?' To answer this question you will need to listen carefully to his word and especially his promises, as well as any intuitions you may receive from the Holy Spirit, as did Uncle Joe in Massachusetts, and Daniel in ancient Babylon.

3. *Prescription*: Having discerned what Satan is trying to do, and what God is wanting to do, ask yourself, 'What can I now do, both prayerfully and practically, to thwart Satan's plan and to welcome God's better purposes into this person, place or situation?'

The passage of Scripture quoted more often than any other in relation to spiritual warfare is Ephesians 6:11–18 in which the Apostle Paul urges us to 'Put on the full armour of God, so that you can take your stand against the devil's schemes.' He proceeds to itemise 'the belt of truth . . . the breastplate of righteousness' . . . the shoes of the gospel '. . . the shield of faith . . . the helmet of salvation and the sword of the Spirit, which is the word of God'.

Wielding the sword of the Spirit

The only piece of military hardware with which we can mount an attack is the word of God. No spears. No flaming arrows. No battering rams. Just the Bible. And this is precisely how we see Jesus fighting the Enemy in the wilderness.[27] He counters every temptation thrown at him with an opposing verse from the Bible. As the writer of Hebrews observes, 'the word of God is alive and active. Sharper than any double-edged sword.'[28] The sword that Paul is describing here is the *gladius*, from which we get our word gladiator: a short blade, between 45 and 68 centimetres long, used by Roman legionaries for close military combat. We are to wield the word of God dextrously, says Paul, in hand-to-hand combat with the Enemy of our souls.

So how do we actually do this? Well, let's say, for example, that a dark cloud of despair descends upon you one morning so that you become inexplicably and overwhelmingly fearful about the future. It occurs to you that these feelings, while powerful, may not be true. You reach for your Bible, find Jeremiah 29:11, and begin to wield it in prayer: 'I know the plans I have for you,' declares the LORD, 'plans to prosper you and not to harm you, plans to give you hope and a future.' Instead of just reading this famous verse and thinking 'how nice', you begin to swing it around your head like a sword. You apply it to your situation, cutting through the Accuser's lies with this sharp truth from God's word. 'I choose to believe that the Lord has a plan for my life and that he's in charge!' you declare aloud. 'I refuse to panic. I'm not going to be afraid. I reject the lie that I'm continually missing out, that everyone else is moving ahead, that I'm getting left behind.' Your mind turns to Romans 8:1: 'There is now no condemnation for those who are in Christ Jesus.' 'Get off my back, Satan,' you say. 'I can see what you're trying to do and I'm not giving in. Stop accusing me. Stop lying to me. I'm seated with Christ in heavenly places. He's on my side. I'm not going to feel guilty or ashamed. I'm clothed in the righteousness of Christ. Get lost!'

'Resist the devil,' says the Apostle James, 'and he will flee from you' (4:7). You will be amazed how powerful this kind of prayerful resistance can be, and how cowardly the Enemy can be when confronted with simple truth in the hands of a believer. One of the reasons that it's important to spend time regularly in the Bible, and especially to memorise verses of Scripture, is that it sharpens your sword. When God speaks to you through his word, it's not just to bring solace to your soul and light to your path, but to arm you with the truth you desperately need for the fight of your life.

I was talking with the Lord one day about a friend who had done something extremely hurtful. I couldn't understand it. It was completely out of character. Part of me wanted to go and confront her. Another part of me wanted just to bury my head in the sand and pretend it hadn't happened. But as I prayed, God helped me to diagnose the problem! The lights went on. Suddenly I could see that her unkindness was driven not by personal animosity but by well-concealed fearfulness in every area of her life. I'd never seen it before, but suddenly it seemed so obvious that many of her behaviours were shaped by a fear of making herself vulnerable, a fear of abandonment, a fear of losing control. With this unexpected diagnosis came a whole new prognosis. 1 John 4:18 says that 'There is no fear in love. But perfect love drives out fear.' Knowing now precisely how to pray, I began to 'drive out fear', rebuking that stronghold of anxiety which was robbing her of so much life and joy. My mind turned to 2 Timothy 1:7 'for the Spirit God gave us does not make us timid, but gives us power, love and self-discipline'.

Carefully I applied each phrase of that verse to her situation. I felt very stirred as I did all of this, as if I was hitting the target, but I was still surprised when she called me soon afterwards to say that God had been speaking to her (I hadn't said anything to her, but he had!). She said that she had suddenly found a new clarity (yes, around the time I'd been praying for her). She felt she needed to say sorry. I believe that turn of heart was triggered in part by the way I had been led to pray, refusing to get bitter but instead listening to the Lord with love for her, resisting the Enemy's strategy to undermine her relationships, and praying instead for his will to be done in her life.

Wearing the shoes of the gospel of peace

As well as the 'sword of the Spirit which is the word of God', Paul says that our feet have been 'fitted with the readiness that comes from the gospel of peace'. The Apostle Peter says something similar: 'Always be prepared to give an answer to everyone who asks you to give the reason for the hope that you have' (1 Pet. 3:15). We are to be in a state of perpetual 'readiness', praying for opportunities so that we can be 'always prepared' to share the Good News. The greatest act of spiritual warfare in the world is when you lead someone into a relationship with Jesus Christ. You will never win a greater victory! It is ultimately 'by the blood of the Lamb and the word of [our] testimony' that we overcome the Enemy. There is nothing he fears more. We must view the word of God, therefore, not just as a sword with which to fight, but also as the shoes in which we march into enemy territory proclaiming the good news of gospel liberation that its citizens have been longing to hear.

It seems ironic that Paul uses a military metaphor to describe 'the gospel of peace', until you remember that he was writing during the *Pax Romana* – a 206-year period of relative stability enforced by Roman rule. In Christ we are called to extend the *Pax Christus* as an army of peace-makers commissioned to convey 'the gospel of peace' to all the earth. Too many of us spend too much of our time spotting all the bad things that the Enemy is doing in our friends, our communities and our countries, when we are meant to be praying and declaring the good things that God has done, is doing and is about to do in our world.

John Wimber, founder of the Vineyard movement, taught that 'it's better to plant seeds than pull weeds', which is such an important principle for spiritual warfare. When I am praying with a person who is under any kind of spiritual attack, I always try to spend more time planting seeds – proactively affirming the good things that I can bless in their lives, rather than pulling weeds – reactively naming and binding the work of Satan.

SOME OF THE MOST POWERFUL WORDS WE CAN POSSIBILY SAY ARE NOT 'IN THE NAME OF JESUS', BUT SIMPLY 'YES' AND 'NO'

The same principle applies to spiritual warfare over a neighbourhood, city or nation. Begin by looking back to discover the historic godly covenants and redemptive gifts that have shaped the host culture over many years. Next, identify any contemporary evidence of God's grace currently at work, and celebrate it with all your might. Finally, look forward with faith for Christ's kingdom to come in this culture, applying God's promises to the place prophetically in prayer. When we lived in Kansas City a number of Christians warned us about certain spiritual strongholds and problems that seemed to prevail in the region. We prayed about these things, and could see that they were real, but we also became obsessed with the fact that we were living in one of the birthplaces of jazz. And so I went to the musicians in our prayer room one day, and asked them, as gently as I could, to stop playing such boring, generic music, and to let rip instead with the kind of joyful, experimental sounds that could serve as an appropriate prophetic celebration of God's gift to and through this great city. Wherever in the world you live, try to spend more time blessing what's right than cursing wrong.[29]

Our words and actions in prayer have far more power than we realise. 'Truly I tell you,' says Jesus, 'whatever you bind on earth will be bound in heaven, and whatever you loose on earth will be loosed in heaven.'[30] Some of the most powerful words we can possibly say, therefore, are not 'in the name of Jesus', but simply 'yes' and 'no'.[31] And Jesus continues, 'Truly I tell you that if two of you on earth agree about anything they ask for, it will be done for them by my Father in heaven.'[32] When it comes to spiritual warfare, power is increased when we agree with other people in prayer. Just as the Roman soldier in Paul's metaphor was only equipped to fight as part of an army, and just as the Lord's Prayer is a plea for deliverance from evil presented entirely in the plural, so we are called to wage war in heaven and peace on earth as part of an army. It's always best to go into battle for breakthrough with others.

Standing our ground

Other than 'the sword of the Spirit' and 'the shoes of the gospel', all the hardware listed in Ephesians 6 is designed for spiritual resistance rather than attack. What's more, in these eight verses, Paul tells the Ephesians repeatedly simply to stand their ground!

> Put on the full armour of God, so that . . . you may be able to *stand your ground*, and after you have done everything, to *stand. Stand firm* then. (Emphasis added)

Paul's emphasis here is clearly on courageous resistance. There is no licence for that common kind of macho militancy that continually (and unwisely) picks fights with the devil in prayer. The Apostle Jude says that 'even the archangel Michael, when he was disputing with the devil . . . *did not himself dare* to condemn him for slander but said, "The Lord rebuke you!"' (Jude v. 9, emphasis added). If the archangel Michael did not dare to rebuke the devil but instead prayed that the Lord would do it, how much more should we beware of arrogance in spiritual warfare. We defy the Enemy best by wielding the word of God humbly, proclaiming the gospel of peace courageously, and living holy lives faithfully in a hostile world.

Standing firm in an opposite spirit

You take a stand against the Enemy every time you preach the gospel, forgive an enemy, stand up to a bully, care for the poor, create something beautiful, behave with integrity, practise civil disobedience for the sake of righteousness, or take a stance that defies his insidious systems of control. For instance, if your office culture is saturated with cynicism, you might model an 'equal but opposite spirit' by speaking words of hope, refusing to gossip, being unusually kind. If there is prejudice and racism in your neighbourhood, you might go out of your way to befriend someone different to yourself. If the churches in your area are divided, you could make a donation to another congregation and commit to pray for its pastor as well as your own.

When 24–7 Prayer sent its first missionaries to Ibiza, Europe's 'party capital', some well-meaning people warned us about the rampant hedonism for which it had become notorious. They quoted the Bible verse about fleeing immorality, and seemed certain that we would inevitably be affected or even infected by all the sin. But we believed something different. We believed that God in us is greater than the gods of this world (1 John 4:4), and so the team committed themselves to radical levels of integrity and accountability in Ibiza, while celebrating the island's God-given beauty and the creativity of its culture. As a result, they managed to live closer to Jesus in a place tagged 'Sodom and Gomorrah' by the media than they might have done back home. It was an act of spiritual defiance on the field of battle, a demonstration of the truth of a simple biblical reality, that 'in all these things we are more than conquerors through him who loved us' (Rom. 8:37).

Towards the end of the twentieth century the great Welsh pastor Martyn Lloyd-Jones wrote a commentary on the book of Ephesians entitled *The Christian Warfare*: 'The history of the present century', he said, 'can only be understood in terms of the unusual activity of the devil and the principalities and powers':

> In a world of collapsing institutions, moral chaos, and increasing violence, never was it more important to trace the hand of the 'prince of the power of the air', and then, not only to learn how to wrestle with him and his forces, but also how to overcome them 'by the blood of the lamb and the word of our testimony'. If we cannot discern the chief cause of our ills, how can we hope to cure them?[33]

* * *

In this chapter, we have surveyed the spiritual warfare that is raging around us, and our extraordinary authority to affect its outcome through militant prayer and practical obedience. We've seen that the reason we need to fight – and indeed the reason for many of our great disappointments in prayer – is that we are living in an era when the tectonic plates are shifting between Christ's resurrection and the day of his return. Like those Thai boys in the cave, we know that we have been saved, and yet we continue to wait patiently and to pray passionately for the day of our complete salvation when 'the kingdom, the power and the glory' will finally come fully and forever.

MORE ON SPIRITUAL WARFARE:

- **PRAYER COURSE SESSION**: #8: Spiritual Warfare (prayercourse.org).

- **PRAYER TOOLS**: 1. Warfare Prayer. 2. How to Fast. 3. How to Prayer Walk (prayercourse.org).

- **FURTHER READING**: *The Screwtape Letters*, by C.S. Lewis.

HERO OF SPIRITUAL WARFARE:

Saint Patrick:
The warrior saint

In his book *How the Irish Saved Civilization*, Thomas Cahill describes the profound transformation brought by Saint Patrick's mission to Ireland. Arriving as a teenage slave, Patrick beheld a country dominated by superstition and druidical paganism at a time when the *Pax Romana* was crumbling and chaos was advancing across Europe. But, by the time he died, Patrick left behind a Christian nation.

'Patrick's gift to the Irish was his Christianity . . . which transformed Ireland into Something New, something never seen before – a Christian culture, where slavery and human sacrifice became unthinkable, and warfare, though impossible for humans to eradicate, diminished markedly.'[34]

For twenty-nine years Patrick worked hard, preaching the gospel and establishing monasteries 'in the midst', as he writes, 'of pagan barbarians, worshipers of idols and unclean things'. It took courage to stand up to the bloodthirsty kings who ruled the land. On one occasion Patrick wrote a furious open letter to King Carroticus demanding that he release his slaves, and commanding him to repent of his sins! But his battle was also spiritual. He describes one particular night, 'when I was asleep, Satan assailed me violently, a thing I shall remember as long as I shall be in this body'.

The key to Patrick's authority and anointing was undoubtedly the prayer life he had first developed as a shepherd boy. 'In one day I said about a hundred prayers, and in the night nearly the same; so that I used even to remain in the woods and in the mountains; before daylight I used to rise to prayer, through snow, through frost, through rain, and I felt no harm; nor was there any slothfulness in me, as I now perceive, because the spirit was then fervent within me' (*Confessions* §16).

The famous prayer attributed to him – St Patrick's breast-plate – is a plea for spiritual protection in the midst of spiritual attack:

> I bind to me these holy powers.
> Against all Satan's spells and wiles,
> Against false words of heresy,
> Against the knowledge that defiles,
> Against the heart's idolatry,
> Against the wizard's evil craft,
> Against the death wound and the burning,
> The choking wave, the poisoned shaft,
> Protect me, Christ, till Thy returning.

The key to Patrick's successful mission, which shaped the destiny of a nation to this day, was the vibrancy and militancy of his prayer life. He inspires us as we seek to fulfil the Great Commission to build our prayer lives, not just our theology, around the victory of Christ.

12: Amen

*'For the kingdom, the power and the glory
are yours, now and forever.'*

———————————

And so the Lord's Prayer finally comes full circle – it lands where
it began. Having started with adoration it concludes with doxology
– with praise. Having 'hallowed' the Father's name, we now declare
his glory. Having prayed for his will to be done, we proclaim his
power. Having invited his kingdom to come, we celebrate that it
has come already, both now and forever more.

These final lines don't feature in the original Gospel renditions, but they've been used to conclude the Lord's Prayer since
the very earliest days of the Church and, significantly, they are
drawn directly from King David, who prayed: 'Yours, LORD, is
the greatness and the power and the glory and the majesty and
the splendour, for everything in heaven and earth is yours.
Yours, LORD, is the kingdom.'[1]

In these carefully chosen words King David is relinquishing
his kingdom, his power and his glory to the King of kings,
giving back to God every blessing he himself has received. We
live in an age when this is rare. We love to speak of 'the kingdom'
without ever really wanting to surrender anything costly to its
King. Our time, our money, our sexual ethics, our achievements,
our dreams for our lives are all resolutely 'ours'. Personal
surrender and costly sacrifice are rare. The kingdom of God is
an unthreatening, ephemeral concept, a vaguely and pleasantly
desirable future prospect, not the kind of concrete present
reality that grazes our knees as we relinquish everything we
cherish to its King.

But to pray these closing lines of the Lord's Prayer is to give the kingdom, the power and the glory back to God. It's to give him our little empires (family, ministry, career) and say 'yours, Lord, is the kingdom'. It's to give him the power-bases we've built and say 'yours, Lord, is the power'. It's to give him our credibility, our trophies of success, and say 'yours, Lord, is the glory forever and right now'.

* * *

As a long-haired student hitchhiking around Europe I received a dramatic vision late one night, on a clifftop in Portugal, of thousands of young people rising out of an atlas. It was an epiphany that eventually gave rise to the 24–7 Prayer movement (and thus the contents of this book), but for nine years I didn't know what to do with it. Nothing happened. God clearly wasn't in any kind of hurry.

When at last the 24–7 movement was born, but before I'd fully grasped that it was the fulfilment of that vision, I was invited to speak at a conference in Valladolid, Spain, and decided to lead the crowd in our war-cry: 'C'mon!' (or '*Venga!*' in Spanish). On this particular night, the packed auditorium just erupted with militant passion. I gazed out in amazement at the sight of a thousand Spanish young people punching the air defiantly, crying out for God's kingdom to come. And as I did so I was transported in my mind to a park bench not far from the venue in which we were meeting. There I saw a long-haired hitchhiker asking: 'Where is the army of young people, Lord?' Immediately I remembered that I had been here before, hitching through Valladolid just days after that vision, trying to make sense of what I'd seen. Fast forward almost a decade and here I was again, and the Holy Spirit was answering my question as if there hadn't been any delay at all: 'Here they are!' he said, as I stared out in amazement at a thousand young people doing a war-cry. 'Here's the army I'm raising.' I was still reeling from that revelation when the Lord told me something else: 'Pete,' he said, 'you need to understand that I never forget a single prayer you pray. You forget most of the things you ask me, but I never do.'

It was true that I'd forgotten visiting this city, let alone asking God that question, but the one for whom 'a thousand years . . . are like a day'[2] had brought me back here now, apparently just to give me an answer. The one who numbers every hair on our heads, and stores every tear that we cry, also remembers every prayer that we pray. This is a mind-blowing truth. If God continues to work towards the fulfilment of our prayers, long after we've forgotten praying them, there must be occurrences and apparent coincidences in your life and mine most days that are direct answers to prayers and questions we don't even remember asking. Our entire lives may be shaped to a very significant extent by the accumulation of such prayers – our own and those of others.

The butterfly effect

The American mathematician Edward Lorenz famously postulated that minor atmospheric disturbances such as the flapping of butterfly wings can eventually alter entire weather patterns. Shouldn't we expect a similar butterfly effect from prayer?

THE ONE WHO NUMBERS EVERY HAIR ON OUR HEADS, AND STORES EVERY TEAR THAT WE CRY, ALSO REMEMBERS EVERY PRAYER THAT WE PRAY

What chain of events might be set in motion by the very next word you say to God? (I imagine fractals spiralling from our lips, smoke rising, rays of light emanating into space.) 'Prayers are prophecies,' says Mark Batterson. 'They are the best predictors of your spiritual future. Who you become is determined by how you pray. Ultimately, the transcript of your prayers becomes the script of your life.'[3]

Perhaps, like the Madagascar Palm, which takes one hundred years to bloom, many of our unanswered prayers are not dead but dormant in the heart of God, awaiting the perfect conditions in which to bear fruit in this life or the next. We pray in days, weeks and months, but he is working for generations to come. 'In the spiritual life God chooses to try our patience first of all by His slowness', said the great hymn-writer Frederick Faber almost two hundred years ago:

> He is slow: we are swift and precipitate. It is because we are but for a time, and He has been from eternity. Thus grace for the most part acts slowly . . . He works by little and by little . . . There is something greatly overawing in the extreme slowness of God. Let it overshadow our souls, but let it not disquiet them . . .
>
> We must wait for God, long, meekly, in the wind and wet, in the thunder and the lightning, in the cold and the dark. Wait, and He will come.[4]

Back to simple

At the start of this book I said that the best advice I ever received about how to pray was to *keep it simple, keep it real* and *keep it up*. Since then, over the subsequent chapters, we've covered a lot of ground, exploring almost every word of the Lord's Prayer together in some detail, and studying nine different aspects of prayer (from centring to spiritual warfare and contemplation to confession). But now it's time to return to the absolute simplicity with which we began.

The heart and soul of prayer is this: the God who made you loves you. He longs to walk and talk with you in ever-deepening friendship. He loves that you've taken time to read this book, because you're wanting to know him better. He doesn't expect you to get it right all the time and understands that some kinds of prayer come more naturally to you than others. Please don't take the techniques and tools I've set out in these pages too seriously. I wouldn't be at all surprised if some of the godliest people in the world have never read a single book about prayer. And sadly, I have certainly met others whose proficiency in prayer belied a hollowness rather than a holiness in their lives.

The great nineteenth-century preacher C.H. Spurgeon said that 'Prayer itself is an art only the Holy Spirit can teach us. Pray for prayer. Pray until you can really pray.' Ultimately we learn to pray by praying – by setting aside time regularly to spend alone with the Lord. And so, if you forget everything else in this book, just remember to P.R.A.Y.! More than anything else, this simple acronym is the thing that will help you grow in prayer.

- '*Pause*'. Remember that crazed greyhound pursued by the bistro chair? Try to 'be still and know' God (Ps. 46:10).
- '*Rejoice* . . . always' (Phil. 4:4). Remember my son Daniel's scribbled prayers? Your Father in heaven loves you, knows you, and interprets your heart perfectly. Give him thanks!
- '*Ask* and it will be given to you' (Matt. 7:7). Remember George Müller praying for daily bread? Ask the Father for everything from peace in the Middle East to parking spaces.
- '*Yield*'. Offer every part of yourself to him as an instrument of righteousness' (Rom. 6:13). Remember those Thai boys trapped in the cave? Wait and trust for the light and hope to come.

One of the most reassuring passages in the whole Bible recognises that we all sometimes find it hard to pray, and promises that the Holy Spirit is here to help us.

> The Spirit helps us in our weakness. We do not know what we ought to pray for, but the Spirit himself intercedes for us through wordless groans. And he who searches our hearts knows the mind of the Spirit, because the Spirit intercedes for God's people in accordance with the will of God. (Rom. 8:26–27)

Isn't that comforting? God isn't marking our prayers with a
scorecard! Our words and techniques don't impress him at all,
but the Holy Spirit 'searches our hearts'. All that really matters,
therefore, is that we bring our hearts before the Father as simply,
honestly and consistently as we can.

Amen

Whenever we say 'Amen' at the end of a prayer we are speaking
an ancient Hebrew word from the Old Testament that was used
in the synagogues, and later adopted by the Church,[5] literally
meaning 'Yes! I agree! So be it!' It's not just a polite way of
signing off a prayer time, but rather an emphatic way of voicing
agreement. This is a powerful thing to do because Jesus promises that 'if two of you on earth agree about anything they ask
for, it will be done for them by my Father in heaven'.[6]

When we say 'Amen' at the end of the Lord's Prayer we are
saying 'yes' to God's Fatherhood and 'count me in' to his family.
We are agreeing with God's people around the world that his
kingdom would come and his will would be done. And together,
as the Apostle Paul puts it, 'the "Amen" is spoken by us to the
glory of God' (2 Cor. 1:20).

In the book of Revelation, John sees twenty-four elders
'holding golden bowls full of incense, which are the prayers of
God's people'. These bowls once full will be poured out at the
end of the Age in a great universal 'Amen'.[7] I find it awesome
to imagine that every true prayer I ever prayed – all the frustrations, the tears, the dashed hopes, and yearnings – are not
wasted, but cherished, remembered by God, stored up in one
of those golden bowls, awaiting their fulfilment. My prayers
for Sammy's healing may not have been fully answered, but
neither have they been forgotten. They are heard and they are
held, awaiting an ultimate answer on the day when brain
tumours and seizures will finally be defeated. Every single time
we say 'Amen', we pull the kingdom a little closer. As theologian
Tim Chester says:

Prayers we think of as directed to the present are in fact being stored up to be answered on the final day. When we pray for those suffering ill health we are expressing our longing for the day when there will be no more sickness (Rev. 21:4). When we pray for God to end wars and oppression we are expressing our longing for the day when the kingdoms of this world will become the Kingdom of our God and of his Christ (Rev. 11:15). When we pray for mercy on those suffering natural disasters we are expressing our longing for the day when creation itself will be remade (Rev. 21:1) . . . The prayers we think have gone unanswered may in fact be stored up in the bowls of incense held by the twenty-four elders, waiting for a greater fulfilment than ever we antici-pated . . . Many of your prayers are lodged there and one day they will determine the ultimate course of history.[8]

One day we will discover that all our praying in this life was just a boot camp for adventures to come. This is just the opening chapter of a much bigger story. We are being trained to exercise authority as Christ's viceroys in a new world, by learning how to partner with him in prayer here in this old one.[9] Like the Karate Kid waxing cars, we are developing character and muscle-memory for greater battles and greater victories to come. When we pray 'hallowed be your name' we are learning to make decisions and reign for his glory. When we pray 'let your kingdom come', we are learning to exercise his authority 'on earth as it is in heaven'.

And so all the things we've been exploring in this book will eventually bring us back full circle to the simple place of *adora-tion* where we began. On that day, other forms of prayer will become redundant. There will no longer be any need for *peti-tion* in the way we now know it because 'before they call I will answer; while they are still speaking I will hear' (Isa. 65:24). We won't need to *intercede* because 'justice [shall] roll on like a river, righteousness like a never-failing stream!' (Amos 5:24). Neither will we wrestle with the pain of *unanswered prayer* because 'there will be no more death or mourning or crying or pain' (Rev. 21:4). *Spiritual warfare* will become unnecessary too because 'the accuser of our brothers and sisters, who accuses them before our God day and night, has been hurled down' (Rev. 12:10). People everywhere will 'beat their swords into ploughshares and their spears into pruning hooks' (Isa. 2:4). The kingdom, the power and glory of God will come in full and 'the earth will be filled with the knowledge of the glory of the LORD as the waters cover the sea' (Hab. 2:14). We'll look around blinking in amazement, and say with C.S. Lewis, 'The term is over: the holidays have begun. The dream is ended: this is the morning.'

The world's prayer

I believe that God has led you to this book because he is calling you to pray, not just to deepen your own personal relationship with him, but also so that you can take your place in a vast, global movement far bigger than me, or the 24–7 movement, or any one personality, programme or brand. We seem to be witnessing one of the greatest mobilisations of prayer the world has ever seen. Thousands upon thousands are gathering in Nigeria, South Africa, China, Brazil, America, Germany, England and many other nations. In Indonesia, entire office blocks are now dedicated to night-and-day prayer. In the Punjab, one prayer centre has led more than thirty thousand people to Jesus. Houses of Prayer are multiplying so fast we can barely keep up. Well over a million people now gather every year in British cathedrals at Pentecost to pray 'Thy Kingdom Come'. The Global Day of Prayer spread from Cape Town into all 220 nations on earth in just eight years. Not so long ago, people in the West had to travel to South Korea to gaze enviously at night-and-day prayer, but it has now become normal here too. And as for those young prayer warriors leaping around shouting '*Venga!*' that night in Valladolid, somehow they have become millions in more than half the nations on earth.

Throughout history, whenever God was about to do a new

thing, he first mobilised his people to pray, and he is currently doing so on an unprecedented scale. What happens next is anyone's guess, but this is undoubtedly an exciting and important time to be learning to pray, seeking to draw closer to the Father, listening to him more carefully, obeying him diligently and beginning to move in greater spiritual authority. One day soon, a trumpet shall sound, the golden bowls of our prayers will be emptied out on the earth, a great 'Amen' will resound in heaven, and Jesus Christ will finally return. When that happens, the Lord's Prayer will become the world's prayer. Every knee will bow before the Father, every tongue will hallow his name, and members of every tribe will lay down their crowns, declaring together that:

The kingdom, the power and the glory are yours,
now and forever.
Amen.

- **PRAYER TOOL**: 1. How to Run a 24–7 Prayer Room (prayercourse.org).

- **FURTHER READING**: *Dirty Glory*, by Pete Greig.

HOW TO USE THIS BOOK
WITH THE PRAYER COURSE

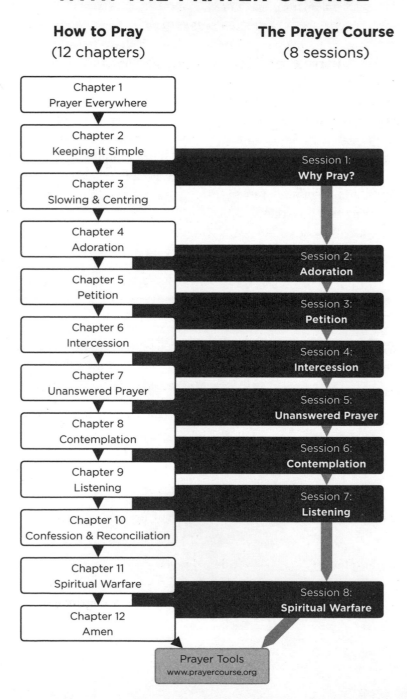

How to Pray
(12 chapters)

The Prayer Course
(8 sessions)

Chapter 1
Prayer Everywhere

Chapter 2
Keeping it Simple

Session 1:
Why Pray?

Chapter 3
Slowing & Centring

Chapter 4
Adoration

Session 2:
Adoration

Chapter 5
Petition

Session 3:
Petition

Chapter 6
Intercession

Session 4:
Intercession

Chapter 7
Unanswered Prayer

Session 5:
Unanswered Prayer

Chapter 8
Contemplation

Session 6:
Contemplation

Chapter 9
Listening

Session 7:
Listening

Chapter 10
Confession & Reconciliation

Chapter 11
Spiritual Warfare

Session 8:
Spiritual Warfare

Chapter 12
Amen

Prayer Tools
www.prayercourse.org

Tool-Shed:

Index of Thirty Prayer Tools

You will find practical introductions to the following topics at www.prayercourse.org:

Notes

Opening quote

1 Martin Luther, tr. Matthew C. Harrison, *A Simple Way to Pray* (St Louis, MO: Concordia, 2012), p. 6.

How to P.R.A.Y.

Chapter 1: Prayer Everywhere

1 Alfred Lord Tennyson, *Idylls of the King*, ed. J.M. Gray (London: Penguin Classics, 1983), p. 288.

2 The eleventh of the Twelve Steps of Alcoholics Anonymous.

3 Abraham Joshua Heschel, *Moral Grandeur and Spiritual Audacity: Essays* (London: Macmillan, 1997), p. 341.

4 David G. Benner, *Opening to God: Lectio Divina and Life as Prayer* (Illinois: IVP Books, 2010), p. 36.

5 This quote was cited by President Obama at the Democratic National Convention, September 2012. It appears to have been first attributed to Abraham Lincoln by Noah Brooks, writing in *Harper's Weekly*, July 1865 (three months after Lincoln's death).

6 Conrad Hilton, *Be My Guest* (New York: Simon & Schuster, 1994), p. 288.

7 Anna Quindlen, *One True Thing* (New York: Random House, 1994), p. 59.

8 Dave Grohl, *This is a Call* (London: HarperCollins, 2012), p. 285.

9 Elizabeth Gilbert, *Eat, Pray, Love* (London: Bloomsbury Publishing, 2007), p. 15.

10 The lines from 'Canal Bank Walk' by Patrick Kavanagh are reprinted from *Collected Poems*, edited by Antoinette Quinn (Allen Lane, 2004), by kind permission of the Trustees of the Estate of the late Katherine B. Kavanagh, through the Jonathan Williams Literary Agency.

11 General Social Survey 2008; C. Bader, K. Dougherty, P. Froese, B. Johnson, F.C. Mencken, J. Park et al., *American Piety in the 21st Century: New Insights to the Depth and Complexity of Religion in the US: Selected Findings from the Baylor Religion Survey* (Waco, TX: Baylor Institute for Studies of Religion, 2016).

12 *Living with the Gods* (London: Allen Lane, 2018), by former Director of the British Museum, Neil MacGregor, chronicles the enduring relevance and surprising increase of religious belief around the world.

13 *Sunday Times*, 17 January 2016, reporting on a 2015 YouGov poll of British beliefs.

14 David Nott was interviewed on *The Eddie Mair Interview* on BBC Radio 4 in 2013 and again in December 2014.

15 Matthew 14:13.

16 Mark 6:46.

17 Matthew 26:36.

18 Matthew 27:46.

19 Acts 1:14.

20 Acts 6:4.

21 Acts 10:9.

22 Acts 9:11.

23 George A. Buttrick, *Prayer* (Abingdon: Cokesbury Press, 1942).

24 Exodus 33:11.

25 John 10:27.

26 Luke 11:1.

27 Matthew 6:6.

28 Acts 2:2–4.

29 To find out more about 24–7 prayer rooms go to www.24-7prayer.com or Tool-shed: *How to Host a 24-7 Prayer Room*.

30 Richard Foster, *Prayer: Finding the Heart's True Home* (London: Hodder & Stoughton, 2008), p. 79.

31 A story recounted by Bill Hybels, former pastor of Willow Creek Community Church.

Chapter 2: Keeping it Simple

1 Psalm 103:14.

2 Matthew 6:6.

3 Samuel Taylor Coleridge, *The Rime of the Ancient Mariner* (New York: Vintage Classics, 2014), p. 32.

4 Matthew 6:7, MSG.

5 This discovery, that the Lord's Prayer originally rhymed, was made by a friend of mine, Bishop Graham Tomlin, as he listened to a Syrian Orthodox priest in Israel reciting the prayer one day, in its original ancient Aramaic form.

6 Archbishop Justin Welby, ChurchofEngland.org.

7 'Dancing Prayers: An Interview with Richard Twiss by Kate Rae Davis', in *The Other Journal: An Intersection of Theology and Culture*, Vol. 21 (The Seattle School of Theology and Psychology; Eugene, OR: Cascade Books, 2013), p. 10.

8 Luke 18:9–12.

9 Thomas Merton, *New Seeds of Contemplation* (New York: New Directions, 1961).

10 Anne Lamott, *Help, Thanks, Wow: The Three Essential Prayers* (London: Hodder & Stoughton, 2015), p. 2.

11 Numbers 11:11–12, MSG.

12 Jeremiah 20:7.

13 C.S. Lewis, *Letters to Malcolm* (London: Geoffrey Bles, 1964), pp. 149–50.

14 Mark 6:31.

15 Eugene Peterson, *Under the Unpredictable Plant* (Grand Rapids, MI: William B. Eerdmans, 1992), p. 74.

16 Mark 1:35.

17 Luke 21:37.

18 Maxwell Maltz postulated in the 1960s that it takes twenty-one days for an activity to become a habit. More recent research at University College, London, into habits of exercise and diet proposes that such habits may take sixty-six days to form.

19 There are many great devotional resources available. My friend and mentor Nicky Gumbel has been using the same devotional routine daily for more than twenty-five years, barely missing a single day, and his insights from these decades of reflection have now been captured in the vastly popular *Bible in One Year* commentary. I also recommend the PRAY365 daily devotional from 24–7 Prayer, *The Divine Hours* trilogy by Phyllis Tickle, *Celtic Daily Prayer* from the Northumbria Community, the *Pray As You Go* podcast from the Irish Jesuits, that perennial classic, *My Utmost for His Highest* by Oswald Chambers, and, of course, *The Book of Common Prayer*.

20 Isaiah 40:31.

STEP 1: PAUSE

Chapter 3: Slowing & Centring

1 Blaise Pascal, *Pensées* (Scotts Valley, CA: CreateSpace, 2011), p. 97.

2 Psalm 42:1.

3 1 Kings 19:12.

4 Psalm 46:10.

5 Richard Rohr, quoting Paula D'Arcy in *Everything Belongs: The Gift of Contemplative Prayer* (New York: Crossroad Publishing, 1999), p. 130.

6 Psalm 37:7.

7 Psalm 46:10.

8 Eugene Peterson, *The Wisdom of Each Other: A Conversation Between Spiritual Friends* (Grand Rapids, MI: Zondervan, 2001), p. 24.

9 Martin Laird, *Into the Silent Land: The Practice of Contemplation* (London: Darton, Longman & Todd, 2006), p. 4.

10 Psalm 131:2.

11 Anthony of the Desert, cited by Thomas Keating, *Open Mind, Open Heart* (London, New York: Continuum, 2007), p. 92.

12 John 20:22.

13 Genesis 2:7.

14 1 Corinthians 14:4.

15 Ed. Evelyn M. Simpson, *John Donne's Sermons on the Psalms and Gospels* (Berkeley, Los Angeles: University of California Press, 1967), p. 226.

16 I am grateful to Brennan Manning for this illustration in his book, *The Signature of Jesus* (Colorado Springs: Multnomah, 1996), p. 218. Used by permission.

17 Brain-Derived Neurotrophic Factor.

18 John 8:6.

19 Matthew 26:39.

20 Athanasius, *The Life of Anthony* (Pickerington, OH: Beloved Publishing, 2014), p. 81.

21 Thomas Merton, *The Wisdom of the Desert: Sayings from the Desert Fathers from the Fourth Century*, sourced in *Emotionally Healthy Spirituality Day by Day*, by Peter Scazzero (Grand Rapids, MI: Zondervan, 2008).

STEP 2: REJOICE

Chapter 4: Adoration

1 David G. Benner, *Opening to God* (Illinois: IVP Books, 2010), p. 26.

2 Jim Wallis and Joyce Hollyday, *Cloud of Witnesses* (Maryknoll, NY: Orbis Books, 1994), p. 6.

3 *Francis of Assisi: The Saint*, Volume 1 (Francis of Assisi: Early Documents) (New York: New City Press, 1999), p. 47.

4 Ephesians 5:1. See also Matthew 7:11.

5 Matthew 7:11.

6 The theme of God's fatherhood, so vital to prayer, is powerfully explored in a number of highly recommended books such as *The Father Heart of God*, by Floyd McClung, *The Return of the Prodigal*, by Henri Nouwen, and *The Cross and the Prodigal: Luke 15 through the Eyes of Middle Eastern Peasants*, by Kenneth Bailey. It is also celebrated in the art and sculpture of my friend Charlie Mackesy.

7 St Augustine's Commentary on Psalm 148 in *Exposition of the Psalms 121–150* (Vol. 6) (New City Press, 2005).

8 Jean-Nicolas Grou, *The Spiritual Life* (Bedford, NH: Sophia Institute Press, 2002), p. 37.

9 Romans 8:26–27.

10 William Barclay, *The Lord's Prayer* (Louisville, KY: Westminster John Knox, 2010), pp. 50-51.

11 Annie Dillard, *Teaching a Stone to Talk* (New York: Harper & Row, 1982), p. 40.

12 Hebrews 10:31.

13 Recounted by Sheldon Vanauken in his memoir *A Severe Mercy* (London: Hodder & Stoughton, 2009), p. 198.

14 George MacDonald, *The Diary of an Old Soul* (New York: Sheba Blake Publishing, 2017), 7 May.

15 Hebrews 13:15.

16 For more information about *The Order of the Mustard Seed* see www. orderofthemustardseed.com.

17 All Jews at Jesus' time would have prayed these fixed prayers. If Jesus had not done so, it would have been noted in Scripture. We find hints of Christ's liturgical practice in his devout attendance of the synagogue, his honouring of the great feasts and festivals, and, for example, Matthew 14:19, in which Jesus gives thanks to God before the feeding of the five thousand.

18 1 Timothy 2:1–2.

19 From an interview with Dr R. Albert Mohler on the *Speaking in Public* broadcast.

20 2 Corinthians 3:18.

21 Exodus 31:1–4. In this passage Bezalel is described as being 'filled with the Spirit of God' – the first person in the Bible to be described in this way – in order to work as a craftsman in the tabernacle.

22 Brother Lawrence, *The Practice of the Presence of God* (London: Hodder & Stoughton, 2009).

STEP 3: ASK

Chapter 5: Petition

1 Cited by Tom Wright, *The Lord and His Prayer* (London: SPCK, 2008), p. 88.

2 1 Thessalonians 5:16–18.

3 John 14:14.

4 Luke 11:9.

5 James 4:2.

6 H.H. Farmer, *The World and God* (London: Nisbet, 1935), p. 129.

7 Karl Barth, *Church Dogmatics III/3*, G.W. Bromiley and T.F. Torrance (eds) (Edinburgh: T&T Clark, 1960), p. 268.

8 The three most important prayers in Jewish liturgy are generally considered to be the *Sh'ma Yisrael* ('Hear, O Israel'), the *Amidah*, and the *Kaddish*.

9 Walter Wink, *Engaging the Powers* (Minneapolis, MN: Fortress, 2017), p. 321.

10 See Roger Steer, *George Müller: Delighted in God* (Wheaton, IL: Harold Shaw, 1981), p. 161.

11 Luke 18:41–43.

12 C.H. Spurgeon, *Spurgeon on Prayer and Spiritual Warfare* (New Kensington, PA: Whitaker House, 1998): 'God will bless Elijah and send rain, but Elijah must pray for it. If the chosen nation is to prosper, Samuel must plead for it. If the Jews are to be delivered, Esther must intercede. God will bless Paul, and the nations shall be converted through him, but Paul must pray . . .'

13 Blaise Pascal, *Pensées* (Scotts Valley, CA: CreateSpace, 2011), p. 63.

14 Karl Barth, *Prayer* (Louisville, KY: Westminster John Knox Press, 2002), p. 21.

15 Richard Foster, *op. cit.*, p. 52.

16 Ephesians 2:18.

17 Matthew 21:22.

18 Matthew 17:20.

19 Hebrews 11:6.

20 Hebrews 12:2.

21 Roger Steer, *J. Hudson Taylor: A Man in Christ* (Mandaluyong City: OMF Books: 1990), p. 298.

22 Luke 18:1–18 .

23 Matthew 7:7 NLT.

Chapter 6: Intercession

1 Walter Wink, *The Powers That Be: Theology for a New Millennium* (New York: Doubleday, 1999), p. 187.

2 Richard Foster, *Prayer: Finding the Heart's True Home* (London: Hodder & Stoughton, 2008), p. 204.

3 This delightful story, recounted by a number of preachers in various forms, is almost certainly apocryphal.

4 1 Timothy 2:2.

5 2 Chronicles 7:14.

6 Exodus 17:11–13.

7 Ephesians 6:12.

8 Cited by Ashley Cocksworth, *Karl Barth on Prayer* (T&T Clark Studies in Systematic Theology 26 (Edinburgh: T&T Clark, 2018), p. 114. Karl Barth himself never included this saying in any of his written works. Its original written source appears to have been his former student Jan Milič Lochman, who heard his teacher use the line on a number of occasions and recounts it in various publications, including *The Lord's Prayer: Perspectives for Reclaiming Christian Prayer*, ed. Daniel L. Migliore (Grand Rapids, MI: Eerdmans, 1993), pp. 18–19.

9 Ezekiel 22:30 (emphasis added).

10 While the story of Exodus 32:9–14 appears to depict God changing his mind in response to Moses' prayers, when it is considered in the light of Christ with an understanding that God's heart is to save and not destroy, and recognising in Moses a 'type' or forerunner of Jesus who intercedes for our salvation, it seems more accurate to conclude that God had wanted Moses to intercede in this way from the start, because his heart was not to destroy but to redeem his people.

11 Hebrews 7:25.

12 John 3:16–17.

13 Romans 8:34.

14 Romans 8:26.

15 Karl Barth, *Church Dogmatics Vol. III*, p. 287.

16 Oswald Chambers, *My Utmost for His Highest* (Grand Rapids, MI: Discovery House, 2017).

17 We are indebted to Jason Mandryk for his encyclopaedic research, compiled in successive editions of the ultimate prayer guide to every nation on earth: *Operation World*, published by IVP.

18 *The Works of President Edwards in Ten Volumes: Vol. III* (New York: S. Converse, 1829), p. 480.

19 2 Corinthians 1:20.

20 Walter Wink, *The Powers that Be: Theology for a New Millennium* (New York: Doubleday, 1999), p. 185.

21 H.E. Dana and J.R. Mantey, *A Manual Grammar of the Greek New Testament* (Toronto, MacMillan, 1927), p. 176.

22 Darrel W. Johnson, *Fifty-Seven Words that Change the World* (Vancouver: Regent College, 2005), p. 20. Some scholars would disagree with Johnson, since the imperative can also be a tone of entreaty, which would lend itself to the context of prayer. Nevertheless, the point stands that we can pray with extraordinary confidence stemming from the *command* of Christ to pray in this way.

23 P.T. Forsyth, *The Soul of Prayer* (Scotts Valley, CA: CreateSpace, 2017), p. 107.

24 Acts 4:24, 31.

25 Sourced in an article in an article in *Christianity Today*, https://www.christianitytoday.com/history/people/denominationalfounders/nikolaus-von-zinzendorf.html.

Chapter 7: Unanswered Prayer

1 Much of the content of this chapter is drawn from my book *God on Mute*, which explores the theme of unanswered prayer in considerably greater detail.

2 John 17:22–23.

3 Matthew 26:38 and Luke 22:44.
4 Mark 14:36.
5 Isaiah 55:8.
6 Philippians 4:6–7.
7 In *God on Mute*, Chapters 7, 8 and 9, I explore this motif – God's world, God's war and God's will – in much greater depth, for those who want to take it a little deeper.
8 The fact that miracles are rare should not discourage us from praying about life's details in the way I advocate in Chapter 5, for the following reasons: 1. It's impossible to know when a thing that appears inconsequential is in fact going to be significant for the future. 2. The obstruction to a particular miracle may be rooted not in the realm of 'God's world' – its natural laws – but in the realm of 'God's war': human freewill and satanic opposition. 3. When we pray about the details and even the inevitabilities of life, we prime ourselves to receive life as a miracle – not least its natural laws – and therefore to live with greater gratitude.
9 C.S. Lewis, *The Problem of Pain* (New York: HarperCollins, 2001), p. 25.
10 Ephesians 6:17.
11 P.T. Forsyth, *The Soul of Prayer* (Scotts Valley, CA: CreateSpace, 2017), p. 14.
12 Tony Reinke, *Newton on the Christian Life* (Wheaton, Il: Crossway, 2015), p. 159.
13 Interview with *Christianity Today*.
14 Joni Eareckson Tada, *When God Weeps*, (Grand Rapids, MI: Zonderuan, 200), p. 117.

STEP 4: YIELD

1 Thomas Merton, *Contemplative Prayer* (London: Darton, Longman & Todd, 1973), p. 13.

Chapter 8: Contemplation
1 T.S. Eliot, *Little Gidding* in *Four Quartets* (London: Folio Society, 1968), pp. 46–7.
2 Elizabeth Bowen
3 *The Life: The Collected Works of St Teresa*, Vol. 1, tr. Kieran Kavanaugh and Otilio Rodriguez (Washington, DC: ICS Publications, 1976), p. 67.
4 David G. Benner, *Opening to God*, p. 117.
5 Richard Foster, *op. cit.*, p. 167.
6 David G. Benner, *op. cit.*
7 2 Corinthians 12:4.
8 Revelation 1:10–12.

9   T. S. Eliot, *op. cit.*

10 Thessalonians 5:17; Ephesians 6:18.

11 This is interesting because Pentecostals and Contemplative traditions tend to think of themselves as being at opposite ends of the ecclesiastical candle, when really they are very similar indeed. Perhaps it's no coincidence that John Wimber, leader of the Vineyard movement and one of the main pioneers of the charismatic renewal of the last century, emerged from a deeply contemplative Quaker background.

12 Patti Smith, *Just Kids* (London: Bloomsbury Paperbacks, 2011), pp. 4–5.

13 This process is developed from language used by Stephen Verney.

14 Rick Warren, *The Purpose Driven Life* (Grand Rapids, MI: Zondervan, 2002), p. 190.

15 Mary Oliver, 'Praying' in *Thirst* (Boston: Beacon Press, 2006), p. 37.

16 Ruth Hayley Barton, *Strengthening the Soul of your Leadership* (Illinois, IVP, 2015), pp. 146–7.

17 Matthew 6:6 (MSG).

18 Stephen Verney, cited by Joyce Huggett, *Listening to God* (London: Hodder & Stoughton, 2005), p. 52.

19 Quoted in Thomas Keating, *Open Mind, Open Heart* (London, New York: Continuum, 2007), p. 92.

20 Austin Kleon, *Steal Like an Artist* (New York: Workman Publishing, 2012), p. 71.

21 2 Corinthians 3:18 (emphasis added).

22 Henri Nouwen, *In the Name of Jesus* (New York: Crossroad, 1989), p. 42.

23 From Mother Teresa's Nobel Lecture, 11 December 1979.

24 Gerard Manley Hopkins, *Poems and Prose* (London: Penguin Classics, 2008), p. 51.

25 Brennan Manning, *op. cit.*, pp. 98–9.

26 Isaac of Stella, as quoted in *The Lord of the Journey: A Reader in Christian Spirituality*, ed. Roger Pooley and Phillip Seddon (London: Collins Liturgical, 1986), p. 36.

27 Blaise Pascal, *Pensées* (Scotts Valley, CA: CreateSpace, 2011), p. 36.

Chapter 9: Listening

1   Søren Kierkegaard, quoted in Richard Foster, *Celebration of Discipline* (London: Hodder & Stoughton, 1989), p. 49.

2   Dietrich Bonhoeffer, *Psalms: The Prayerbook of the Bible* (Minneapolis, MN: Augsburg Fortress, 1959), p. 11.

3   Malachi 3:16.

4   Matthew 4:4.

5   2 Timothy 3:16.

6   Hebrews 4:12.

7   Mark Batterson, *The Circle Maker* (Grand Rapids, MI: Zondervan, 2012),
    p. 94.
8   1 Corinthians 14:29.
9   1 Kings 19:13.
10 Luke 2:19.
11 2 Corinthians 5:7.
12 Isaiah 30:21.
13 Amy Carmichael, *If* (US: Popular Classics, 2012), p. 26.

Chapter 10: Confession & Reconciliation

1   Frederick Buechner, *Wishful Thinking: A Theological ABC* (London:
    HarperCollins, 1987), p. 1.
2   Stanley Hauerwas was declared 'America's Best Theologian' by *Time*
    magazine in 2010! This quote comes from a book he wrote with William
    H. Willimon, *Lord, Teach Us: The Lord's Prayer and the Christian Life*
    (Nashville, TN: Abingdon Press, 1996), p. 78.
3   William Shakespeare, *King Lear*, Act 1, scene ii.
4   William Barclay, *The Beatitudes and the Lord's Prayer for Everyman* (New
    York: Harper & Row, 1963), p. 227.
5   Paul Vallely, *Pope Francis: Untying the Knots* (London, New York:
    Bloomsbury Continuum, 2015), p. 124.
6   1 John 1:9.
7   Charles W. Colson, *Born Again* (Grand Rapids, MI: Chosen Books, 2008),
    pp. 125, 129.
8   Fr Dennis Hamm SJ, of Creighton University.
9   David G. Benner, *op. cit.*, p. 153.
10 Genesis 3:8.
11 Luke 18:11, 13–14.
12 2 Corinthians 3:18.
13 Matthew 5:23–24.
14 Russell Brand, *Recovery: Freedom from our Addictions* (London: Pan
    Macmillan, 2018), p. 94.
15 See 1 John 4:20.
16 From Robert Coles, *The Story of Ruby Bridges* (New York: Scholastic, 2004)
    and assorted interviews conducted by both Coles and Bridges herself.
17 Luke 23:34.
18 Michael Ramsden in private conversation.
19 Matthew 5:44.
20 2 Corinthians 5:18.
21 Matthew 18:22.
22 William L. Ury, *The Third Side: Why We Fight and How We Can Stop*
    (London: Penguin Putnam, 2000), p. 167.

Chapter 11: Spiritual Warfare

1 C.S. Lewis, *Mere Christianity* (London: Geoffrey Bles, 1953), p. 37.

2 V. Raymond Edman, *They Found The Secret* (Grand Rapids, MI: Zondervan, 1984), p. 179.

3 Joel S. Woodruff, 'Profile in Faith: V. Raymond Edman', in *Knowing & Doing, Journal of the C.S. Lewis Institute*, winter 2011.

4 Ephesians 6:12.

5 C.S. Lewis, *Christian Reflections* (London: HarperCollins, 2017), p. 33.

6 John 10:10.

7 Bruce Cockburn, 'Lovers in a Dangerous Time', from the album *Stealing Fire* (True North, Gold Mountain, A&M, 1984).

8 Martin Luther, *Luther's Works*, Vol. 54 (Minneapolis, MN: Fortress, 1967), p. 94.

9 1 Corinthians 12:10.

10 Andrew Delbanco, *The Death of Satan: How Americans Have Lost the Sense of Evil* (New York: Farrar, Straus and Giroux, 1995).

11 Helmut Thielicke, *Our Heavenly Father: Sermons on the Lord's Prayer*, (New York: Harper and Brothers, 1960), p. 133.

12 'Humankind is losing faith in the liberal story that dominated politics in recent decades, exactly when the merger of biotech and infotech confronts us with the biggest challenges humankind has ever known.' Yuval Noah Harari, *21 Lessons for the 21st Century* (London: Jonathan Cape, 2018).

13 Matthew 4:3.

14 Luke 10:18.

15 Matthew 12:22–32; Matthew 16:18; Mark 3:20–30; Luke 10:19; Luke 11:14–26.

16 Luke 22:31–32.

17 Tom Wright, *The Lord and His Prayer* (London: SOCK, 1996), p. 71.

18 One of the theologians who's written most extensively about our battle against 'principalities and powers' is Walter Wink, particularly in his book *Engaging the Powers*, which I would encourage you to read if you want to understand this topic at a deeper level.

19 Daniel 10:12–13.

20 William H. Willimon and Stanley Hauerwas, *Lord, Teach Us: The Lord's Prayer and the Christian Life* (Nashville, TN: Abingdon, 1996), p. 89.

21 The word 'Christian' only appears three times in the biblical text – as a nickname in Acts 11:26, Acts 26:28 and 1 Peter 4:16 – and is never used by Paul.

22 My emphasis here is upon sharing in the power of Christ, and therefore in the agenda of Christ, rather than exercising power in and of ourselves. This is in contrast to the prosperity gospel as well as the notion that everything is a spiritual enemy.

23 Tom Wright, *op. cit.*, p. 72.

24 Chuck Lowe, *Territorial Spirits and World Evangelization* (Littleton, CO: OMF Books, 1998), p. 70.

25 John Piper, 'Prayer: The Work of Missions', ACMC Annual Meeting, Denver, Colorado, 28 July 1988.

26 2 Kings 6:17.

27 Mark 1:12–13; Matthew 4:1–11; Luke 4:1–13.

28 Hebrews 4:12.

29 Jesus understood the power of cursing (e.g. the fig tree, Matthew 21:19) and permitted his disciples to sometimes use its power (Luke 9:5, Matthew 18:18), but his onus is towards blessing. He commands his followers 'bless those who curse you and pray for those who ill-treat you' (Luke 6:28). Also see James 3:9.

30 Matthew 18:18.

31 Matthew 5:37.

32 Matthew 18:19.

33 Martyn Lloyd-Jones, Introduction to *The Christian Warfare: An Exposition of Ephesians 6:10–13* (Grand Rapids: Baker, 1998).

34 Thomas Cahill, *How the Irish Saved Civilization* (London: Sceptre, 1995), p. 148.

Chapter 12: Amen

1 1 Chronicles 29:11.

2 Psalm 90:4.

3 Mark Batterson, *op. cit.*, p. 14.

4 Father Faber, *Growth in Holiness* (Charlotte, NC: TAN Books, 2009) pp. 145, 149.

5 For the use of the word 'Amen' in the Old Testament see 1 Kings 1:36; Numbers 5:22; Deuteronomy 27:17–26.

6 Matthew 18:19.

7 Revelation 5:8.

8 Tim Chester, *The Message of Prayer* (Downers Grove, IL: IVP, 2003), p. 243.

9 The call to rule with Christ is a theme throughout Scripture, beginning in Genesis 1:26, KJV ('Let them have dominion over . . . all the earth'), continuing through the Abrahamic and Davidic covenants, fulfilled in Christ's Great Commission ('Go . . . make disciples of nations'), enforced in the Pauline epistles such as 1 Corinthians 6:3 (we are to 'judge the angels'), Ephesians 2:6 ('God raised us up with Christ and seated us with him in the heavenly realms'), 2 Timothy 2:12 ('we will also reign with him') and so on.

Further Reading and Recommended Resources

There are thousands of books on prayer but these are some of the titles I recommend:

General books on prayer
Letters to Malcolm, Chiefly on Prayer, by C.S. Lewis
Prayer: Finding the Heart's True Home, by Richard Foster
The Circle Maker, by Mark Batterson
With Christ in the School of Prayer, by Andrew Murray

Personality and prayer
Sacred Pathways, by Gary Thomas

Perseverance and unanswered prayer
A Grief Observed, by C.S. Lewis
Luminous Dark, by Alain Emerson
God on Mute, by Pete Greig

Intercession and spiritual warfare
Mountain Rain: A Biography of James O. Fraser, by Eileen
   Crossman
The Soul of Prayer, by P.T. Forsyth
The Screwtape Letters, by C.S. Lewis
Shaping History Through Prayer and Fasting, by Derek Prince

Contemplation and listening to God
Opening to God, by David G. Benner
Into the Silent Land: The Practice of Contemplation, by
   Martin Laird

The Practice of the Presence of God, by Brother Lawrence
Hearing God, by Dallas Willard
The Sacred Year, by Michael Yankoski

The Lord's Prayer
The Lord's Prayer, by William Barclay
Fifty-Seven Words that Changed the World, by Darrell W.
    Johnson
Praying the Lord's Prayer, by J.I. Packer
The Lord and His Prayer, by Tom Wright

Devotional resources
My Utmost for His Highest, by Oswald Chambers
Common Prayer: A Liturgy for Ordinary Radicals, by Shane
    Claibourne et al.
The Bible in One Year (app), by Nicky and Pippa Gumbel
Operation World: The Definitive Prayer Guide to Every Nation,
    ed. Jason Mandryk
Celtic Daily Prayer, by The Northumbria Community
The Divine Hours Series, by Phyllis Tickle

With Thanks To

This book has been a team effort reflecting the best part of twenty years. There's no way I'd have made it without the support (wisdom, friendship, prayers and frequent ribbing) of our leadership teams at both 24-7 International and Emmaus Rd – Adam, Bill, Brian, Carla, Hannah, Ian, Jill, Joe, Mike, Misty, Nick, Phil, Roger, Sammy, Scot, Wardy. One of the most important people in the process has been Holly Donaldson (née Dobson), whose faithful daily assistance and consistent encouragement has made this entire project less impossible. Alain Emerson did a masterful job pulling together the Thirty Prayer Tools and many of this book's Prayer Heroes too. Three lovely couples also provided me with boltholes in which to write – Gill and Peter on The Island, Helen and Paul at Corfe Castle, Dave and Jo in Turkey. I can't thank you all enough for your kindness. I am also deeply grateful to my nine brilliant readers whose feedback upgraded the content immeasurably: Carla Harding, Hudson Greig, Jill Weber, Joanna Callander, Mark Knight, Nick Beasley, Phil Togwell, Simon Benham and Robbie Back (who somehow managed to read the manuscript in the back of a van while touring Europe with his thrash metal band). Any remaining typos, bloopers, boring bits or dark heresies are mine, not theirs.

My publishing teams on both sides of the pond have been exceptional: Katherine Venn kept me supplied with Scooby Snacks, wise advice and unstinting encouragement; David Zimmerman threatened to send me David Bowie playlists and grasped jokes no one else could understand; and Don Pape has literally wept over this manuscript while praying through its process of formation with his wife Ruthie. Publishers are the great unsung heroes of the book-making business, and although their work impacts on millions of lives it does so quietly and humbly. Katherine, David and Don are some of the finest artisans of Caxton's craft anywhere in the world, and I am very grateful to them for turning the coffee-powered ruminations of a scruffy Brit into something much better-looking and far more sensible than its author.

THE
PRAYER COURSE

How to Pray has been specially designed to accompany The Prayer Course, an eight-session journey through the Lord's Prayer used by thousands of churches and small groups. This free online resource includes:

INTERVIEWS
A series of short videos presented by Pete Greig exploring different aspects of prayer.

TOOL-SHED
A valuable archive of practical 'Prayer Tools' covering topics as diverse as 'How to Fast', 'How to Have a Quiet Time' and 'How to Run a Non-boring Prayer Meeting'.

CHEAT SHEETS
Downloadable discussion-starters for group leaders to aid deep conversation and personal application of each topic.

THE SESSIONS

SESSION 1
Why Pray?
—

SESSION 2
Adoration
—

SESSION 3
Petition
—

SESSION 4
Intercession

SESSION 5
Unanswered Prayer
—

SESSION 6
Contemplation
—

SESSION 7
Listening
—

SESSION 8
Spiritiual Warfare

www.**prayercourse**.org

CREATED BY 24-7 PRAYER

Pete Greig is one of the founding champions of the 24-7 Prayer movement, and serves as the Senior Pastor of Emmaus Rd in Guildford, England. He is an Ambassador for the NGO Tearfund, an Associate Tutor at St Mellitus Theological College in London, and a member of The Order of the Mustard Seed. Pete hosts two major British festivals: Wildfires and The Big Church Day Out.

His books which are available in a range of languages and formats (including audio), are available from all the usual outlets and include the following titles:

Red Moon Rising	God on Mute	Dirty Glory
Rediscovering the Power of Prayer (Red Moon Chronicles #1)	*Engaging the silence of Unanswered Prayer*	*Go Where Your Best Prayers Take You (Red Moon Chronicles #2)*

Stay connected with Pete:

WWW.PETEGREIG.INFO